Designing Digital Computer Systems with Verilog

This book serves both as an introduction to computer architecture and as a guide to using a hardware description language (HDL) to design, model and simulate real digital systems. The book starts with an introduction to Verilog: the HDL chosen for the book since it is widely used in industry and straightforward to learn. Next, the instruction set architecture (ISA) for the simple VeSPA (Very Small Processor Architecture) processor is defined; this processor has been simulated and thoroughly tested at the University of Minnesota by the authors. The VeSPA ISA is used throughout the remainder of the book to demonstrate how behavioral and structural models can be developed and intermingled in Verilog. Although Verilog is used throughout, the lessons learned will be equally applicable to other HDLs. Written for senior and graduate students, this book is also an ideal introduction to Verilog for practicing engineers. A companion website is available with the Verilog source code for all of the examples in the text, Verilog source code for the VeSPA processor, and additional software to assist in using the VeSPA simulations. See www.cambridge.org/9780521828666 for details.

DAVID LILJA is a professor of electrical and computer engineering, and a fellow of the Minnesota Supercomputing Institute, at the University of Minnesota in Minneapolis. He also serves as a member of the graduate faculties in computer science and scientific computation, and was the founding director of graduate studies for computer engineering. He has served on the program committees of numerous conferences and as associate editor for IEEE Transactions on Computers. David is a senior member of the IEEE and a member of the ACM.

SACHIN SAPATNEKAR is the Robert and Marjorie Henle Professor in the Department of Electrical and Computer Engineering at the University of Minnesota, and serves on the graduate faculty in computer science and engineering. He has served as associate editor for several IEEE journals, and has been a distinguished visitor for the IEEE Computer Society, and a distinguished lecturer for the IEEE Circuits and Systems Society. He is a recipient of the NSF Career Award and the SRC Technical Excellence Award. He is a fellow of the IEEE and a member of the ACM.

Designing Digital Computer Systems with Verilog

David J. Lilja and Sachin S. Sapatnekar
Department of Electrical and Computer Engineering
University of Minnesota
Minneapolis

CAMBRIDGE UNIVERSITY PRESS
Cambridge, New York, Melbourne, Madrid, Cape Town, Singapore, São Paulo

Cambridge University Press
The Edinburgh Building, Cambridge CB2 8RU, UK

Published in the United States of America by Cambridge University Press, New York

www.cambridge.org
Information on this title: www.cambridge.org/9780521828666

First published 2005
This digitally printed version (with corrections) 2007

A catalogue record for this publication is available from the British Library

Library of Congress Cataloguing in Publication data

Lilja, David J.
  Designing digital computing systems with Verilog/David J.Lilja and Sachin S. Sapatnekar.
    p.   cm.
  Includes bibliographical references and index.
  ISBN 0 521 82866 X (alk. paper)
    1. Verilog (Computer hardware description language) 2. Electronic digital computers – Design and
Construction. I. Sapatnekar, Sachin S., 1967 – II. Title.

TK7885.7.L55 2005
621.39'2 – dc22   2004054515

ISBN 978-0-521-82866-6 hardback
ISBN 978-0-521-04572-8 paperback

Contents

Preface

To the engineer, all matter in the universe can be placed into one of two categories: (1) things that need to be fixed, and (2) things that will need to be fixed after you've had a few minutes to play with them.

Quoted by Scott Adams in The Dilbert Principle.

Hardware description languages (HDLs) are used extensively in industry to design digital systems ranging from microprocessors to components within consumer appliances, such as cellular telephones. These languages allow engineers to quickly and precisely specify and document their designs in a high-level language that has strong similarities to conventional programming languages, such as Java, C, and C++. Automatic tools exist to simulate the design using this high-level description and, ultimately, to translate the design from the hardware description language into an actual silicon chip.

There are two primary hardware description languages in use by industry today, Verilog and VHDL. Both languages solve the same basic problem, but in slightly different ways. There are strong adherents to both languages and arguments about which is better often seem to have the feel of a religious war. The Institute of Electrical and Electronic Engineers (IEEE) made Verilog an international standard in 1995 and it continues to be refined and enhanced.

Numerous books have been written to describe both languages. These books range from the IEEE standards document, to tutorial texts that introduce the language to novices, to texts for advanced users that describe the many subtle aspects of the languages. However, these books tend to treat the languages as just another programming language to be learned. They tend to miss the forest for the trees since they fail to view the broader goals of design as they focus on the details of describing specific circuits rather than considering the larger picture that encompasses architectural choices and their impact on circuit design, and vice versa.

The philosophy behind this book is to view the language as only a tool in the overall design process used to produce the final product, which is the piece of silicon that is a part of a larger system. This book will teach the reader how to design a complex digital system using the Verilog HDL as the vehicle for modeling and simulating the design. We have chosen to focus on Verilog due to its economic importance and due to its popularity and widespread use among the designers of processors and other digital systems within the computing industry. Our philosophy is to teach the components of the language that are necessary for the design of our example processor simultaneously with the teaching of the overall design process.

Organization

This book begins with a brief introduction to the hierarchical design process that is used throughout the book to control the complexity involved in designing a large-scale digital system. Chapter 2 then introduces the Verilog language using several relatively small examples. The instruction set architecture (ISA) for the simple VeSPA processor is defined in Chapter 3 along with a running commentary explaining the reasoning behind the various trade-offs that must be made during the design of any system. This ISA is used throughout the remainder of the book to demonstrate how a behavioral model of the processor can be developed (Chapter 4) and then refined into a detailed pipelined implementation (Chapter 7). Along the way, we describe how an assembler is constructed to translate assembly language programs into machine language (Chapter 5) and the general concepts involved in pipelining a processor design (Chapter 6). The book concludes with a discussion of several techniques that are used to verify the correctness of the final design (Chapter 8). Appendix A provides a concise summary of the VeSPA instruction set, while Appendix B presents the details of the VeSPA assembler.

At the end of some chapters, we provide suggestions for further reading for those who are interested in pursuing a particular topic in more detail. There is also a companion web site for this book (see www.cambridge.org/9780521828666 for details) with the Verilog source code for all of the examples used in the book, plus some additional tools that can be used with the VeSPA processor models, such as the assembler.

Suggestions for using this text

This book was written primarily with the following three uses in mind:

1. **As a supplemental text for an undergraduate course in computer architecture.** Popular existing computer architecture textbooks tend to base their discussions around simple processors designed specifically for the needs of the given textbook. What these books often fail to do, however, is to tie the overall design process into the hardware description language methodology that engineers actually use in industry. This book provides a useful supplement to a computer architecture course to show how a hardware description language is actually used to design

a processor from start to finish. For example, a course instructor could assign students the task of modifying the VeSPA processor presented in this book as a series of homework assignments throughout the term.

2. **As the primary text for a computer design laboratory course.** This book would be useful as the text for a computer design laboratory course. This type of course may be offered independently, or as a formal component of a computer architecture course, as suggested above.

3. **As a self-teaching guide for graduate engineers.** The book has a very tutorial flavor. This approach makes it useful for practicing engineers who want a self-study text to update their skills in the area of digital systems design. It would also be appropriate for someone who knows VHDL, for instance, but needs to learn Verilog.

Acknowledgements

The development of any book requires the efforts of more than just the authors. And this book is no exception.

We would particularly like to acknowledge the contributions of Saurabh Dighe to the design of the pipelined implementation of VeSPA presented in Chapter 7. Saurabh also provided substantial help in generating the figures used in this chapter.

We also would like to thank Jerry Sobelman for his careful reading of an early draft of the book, and his courage in using this draft while teaching a course on computer organization and design. He pointed out numerous errors and confusing explanations, which we hope we have corrected satisfactorily.

The numerous students who muddled through our very early attempts at teaching our computer organization course using some rather raw versions of the VeSPA design and this text deserve both our apologies and sincere thanks. Their suggestions and feedback helped us improve both the processor design and our writing.

Finally, we thank the anonymous reviewers of our original proposal to develop this book for their insightful comments and specific suggestions for focusing some of the explanations and discussion.

While all of these people made substantial contributions to the outcome of this book, any errors that remain are our responsibility.

1 Controlling complexity

Technical skill is mastery of complexity while creativity is mastery of simplicity.

E. Christopher Zeeman, Catastrophe Theory, 1977

The goal of this text is to teach you how to design a processor from scratch. In a step-by-step process, we will teach you how to specify, design, and test a processor as an example of a complex digital system. We will use the commercially important Verilog hardware description language (HDL) as the basis for this design process.

In particular, we will develop the VeSPA (*Very Small Processor Architecture*) processor as a vehicle for demonstrating the overall design process. We show how the instruction set for this processor is defined, how to build an assembler for the processor, how to develop a behavioral simulator in Verilog to test the instruction set and the assembler, and how to develop a complete Verilog structural model of a pipelined implementation of the processor. We also describe the synthesis process for automatically translating this structural model into a real piece of silicon hardware. We end by demonstrating several techniques that can be used to verify the correctness of the processor design.

1.1 Hierarchical design flow

The development of any type of digital computing system is fundamentally a problem of controlling complexity. The designer of a large-scale digital system, such as a processor, begins with a high-level idea of what tasks the system is to perform. To realize this system in some physical technology, such as a collection of VLSI (Very Large-Scale Integrated circuit) silicon chips, the designer must determine how millions of individual transistors should be interconnected to perform the desired operations. The need to translate from a high-level conceptual view of the system to a specification of the complex interconnections among a virtual sea of transistors is referred to as the designer's *abstraction gap*, as suggested in Figure 1.1.

To bridge this gap between system concept and physical realization, we can use the *hierarchical design flow* process shown in Figure 1.2. The *instruction set architecture*

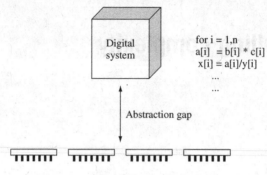

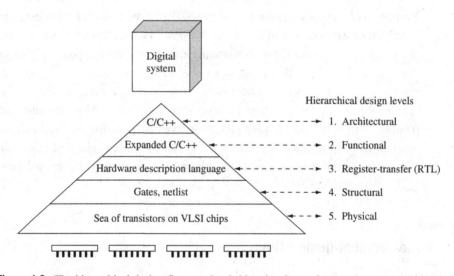

Figure 1.1. The need to translate from the high-level conceptual view of a digital system, such as a processor capable of executing the program shown above, to its physical realization in VLSI chips leads to the designer's abstraction gap.

Figure 1.2. The hierarchical design flow used to bridge the abstraction gap between the high-level view of a digital system and its physical realization in VLSI chips.

(ISA) specification at the highest level in this design hierarchy provides an abstract description of what functions the system is capable of performing. In the case of the design of a processor, this level specifies the instructions available to the assembly language programmer and the programmer-visible architectural storage elements, such as the general-purpose registers, the program counter, and the processor status register. This level of the hierarchy is typically described using a written assembly language programmer's manual.

The *behavioral* level of the design hierarchy is a logical refinement of the ISA specification. This level provides precise functional information about how the system's state is affected by each of the operations specified in the ISA. The behavioral Verilog model developed in this step can actually execute machine language programs written for the processor. However, it typically contains no timing information showing how long each instruction takes to execute, nor does it specify how the operations are implemented. It is used to verify that the ISA is defined correctly, and to provide a simulator on which programmers, such as compiler writers and operating system programmers, can begin developing and testing their code.

This *behavioral* level in the design hierarchy is sometimes referred to as the *register-transfer level* (RTL) since it describes transformations that occur to the contents of registers as they are moved among the storage elements defined by the ISA. However, it does not typically specify how the transformation itself is implemented. For instance, the subtraction of the contents of register rs2 from the contents of register rs1 with the results stored in register rdst may be specified at this level in Verilog as R['rdst] = R['rs1] − R['rs2]. This RTL or behavioral description shows *what* happens in a subtraction operation, but it does not specify *how* it happened or how much time was required.

The next level in the design hierarchy is the *structural* level. This level begins to answer the questions of how a function is actually implemented. It also begins to define the number of cycles required to execute each operation, the number of buses that interconnect registers and functional units, the size of internal memory buffers, and so forth. This level represents a mapping of the behavioral model into a more specific implementation. For example, this level defines how the subtractor actually performs a subtraction operation.

Finally, the *physical* design level specifies the detailed chip-level floor-planning, layout, and transistor-level timing. It defines a mapping of the structural level description on to a specific technology, such as a CMOS application-specific integrated circuit (ASIC). This final stage in the design hierarchy often can be produced automatically from the structural Verilog description using an appropriate logic synthesis design automation tool. The designer may choose to translate certain portions of the design from the behavioral or structural level to the next level by hand, however, to optimize specific design criteria, such as power consumption, chip area, or signal delays, for instance.

Since each level in this design hierarchy is an incremental refinement of the previous level, this hierarchical design flow provides a technique for managing the complexity of designing a large digital system. The hardware description language is a means for precisely capturing the details at the behavioral and structural levels of the design hierarchy. These behavioral and structural models can be compiled and simulated to verify the correctness of the design at each level. The structural model then provides the input for a synthesis tool that will make the final transformation of the hardware description language model into a piece of silicon.

1.2 Designing hardware with software

Using the above design flow, it can often seem that designing a processor is very much like writing a piece of software. Indeed, both the behavioral and structural models of a processor are written in the hardware description language and can be changed, compiled, and executed (actually, simulated) in a manner very similar to writing, compiling, and executing a program written in a high-level programming language, such as C, C++, Java, or Fortran, for instance. However, it is important to distinguish the fundamental differences in this hardware design process from the process of writing software to run on a processor.

Figure 1.3 shows how a hardware designer begins with the ISA, develops a functional and behavioral model, refines these models into a structural model, and, finally, synthesizes that model into the actual processor. This processor consists of hardware storage elements for the ISA-defined registers, logic circuits that implement the ISA-specified instructions, and the memory system. In the final step, it is a real, tangible piece of hardware. To change the processor, for instance, to add a new instruction, every step in this chain of events must be repeated. The result is a new silicon chip with the additional logic circuits necessary to implement this new instruction. While it may be quite simple to make the changes necessary to implement this new instruction in the ISA specification manual and the Verilog models, it can be a slow and expensive process to actually fabricate the new chip.

The analogous process for compiling and executing a program written in a high-level language is compared to this hardware design process in Figure 1.4. A programmer begins with a logical description of the task to be accomplished by the program. This description is refined into an algorithm that describes the steps

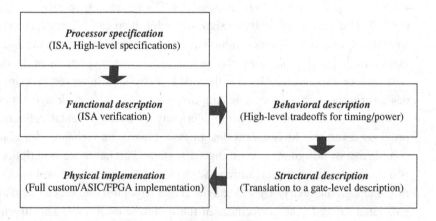

Figure 1.3. The process of refining the behavioral and structural models in a hardware description language to produce a new processor.

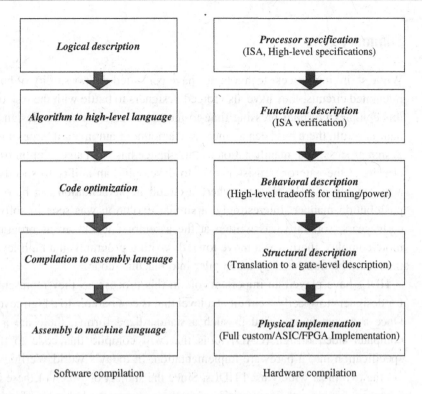

Figure 1.4. The process of compiling and executing a program to run on an existing processor has strong similarities to the process of designing a digital system using a hardware description language. However, the final results of the two processes are quite different.

necessary to complete the desired task. This algorithm then is written in a textual format in the syntax of some high-level language, such as C/C++. A compiler reads this text file and transforms the program into another text file containing an equivalent program in the target processor's assembly language. Finally, this text file is read by an assembler and converted into a string of bits that can be linked with other precompiled library functions and loaded into the processor's memory. At this point, the processor can execute the program stored in its memory.

Changing anything in the program requires each of these steps to be repeated beginning with the text file that contains the modified high-level program. However, in contrast to the need to produce a new silicon chip, the recompiled program can simply be loaded into the processor's memory where it is ready to be re-executed. While the steps required to produce the processor chip are analogous to those required to compile and execute a program, the last step in each process produces completely different results. The software compilation process produces a string of bits that are stored in the processor's memory. The hardware development process, however, ultimately produces a new artifact in the form of a new piece of silicon.

1.3 Summary

While shrinking process technologies have permitted the possibility of building large integrated circuits, they have also forced designers to battle with the task of managing this complexity under pressing time-to-market constraints on the design cycle. As a natural result, there has been an increased amount of automation throughout the entire design process. One manifestation of this change has been an evolution from building circuits at the gate or transistor level to developing an ability to specify circuits at a reasonably high level, from where a circuit implementation can be obtained in a push-button manner. Interestingly, a similar evolution was seen in software: in the early years, software was written at the assembler level, but as programs became more complex, there was a move towards writing programs in a high-level language that could be translated by a compiler into machine code.

HDLs have played an important role in this process, as they represent a medium for designers to specify a circuit at a level that is comparable to a high-level language. Once a design is specified in such a standardized format, there are a number of computer-aided design (CAD) tools that will compile this code to translate the specification into a hardware implementation. In today's world, Verilog and VHDL are the two most widely used HDLs. Since the subject of which of these is the better language can prompt fierce partisan reactions among the believers of either sect, we will prudently avoid that debate.[1] In this book, we use the Verilog HDL as a vehicle for processor design, and our rationale for this choice is threefold. Firstly, we feel that Verilog, being more C-like, is easier for the novice to learn, and is less encumbered with syntactic niceties than VHDL. Secondly, it is arguably the most widely used HDL in industry today. Thirdly, and we believe, most convincingly, learning Verilog provides an easy path to learning any other HDL, and the major goal of this book is to profess the ideas behind processor design using HDLs, rather than to evangelize any specific HDL.

---

[1] A third prong to the debate may be added in the near future with the advent of newer hardware description languages based on C, although these are in the early stages of use at this time.

2 A Verilogical place to start

Let's start at the very beginning.
A very good place to start.
When you read, you begin with A-B-C,
when you sing, you begin with Do-Re-Mi.

from Rogers and Hammerstein's The Sound of Music

In this chapter, we will present an elementary introduction to Verilog, with the primary aim of permitting the reader to learn enough of the language to carry out a competent design. Due to the scope of this text, we do not attempt to present complete coverage of the language; for example, we will not cover switch-level modeling concepts that are typically at the transistor-level, since the design of our processor does not require that level of design detail. For these and other details, the interested reader may refer to sources such as those shown in the *Further reading* section at the end of this chapter.

2.1 My Veri first description

In teaching an English-speaker a new tongue such as Spanish or Japanese or Marathi, two extreme approaches may be attempted. A more structured approach would lead the student through a rigorous path that first teaches the alphabet, followed by words, sentences and grammar; an alternative 'immersive' or 'communicative' approach places the student in an environment where the language is extensively spoken, in the hope that this may motivate learning in a more natural environment. In practice, of course, an intermediate approach is often the most effective, and we will use a similar philosophy in presenting a first exposition to the admittedly nonhuman language that is Verilog.

In this section, we will present a simple Verilog description of a very simple module. The module that we present is a full adder that inputs three bits, the addend bits, a and b, and the input carry bit, c_{in}. The full adder outputs two bits, the sum bit, s, and the output carry bit, c_{out}, and these are related by the elementary equations

$$s = a \oplus b \oplus c_{in}$$

$$c_{out} = a \cdot b + a \cdot c_{in} + b \cdot c_{in}$$

A Verilog description is shown in Figure 2.1, and is fairly self-explanatory. The description is encapsulated within a `module` that is parameterized by its *ports*, or connections to the external world. The body of the module first declares these parameters as inputs or outputs, followed by a description that defines the functionality of the module in terms of its logic equations; note that the symbols ^, & and | refer to the XOR, AND and OR logical operators, respectively.

```
module full_adder(a,b,cin,s,cout);

  input a,b,cin;      // declaration of the list of inputs
  output s, cout;     // declaration of the list of outputs

  assign s = a ^ b ^ cin;
  assign cout = (a & b) | (a & cin) | (b & cin);

endmodule
```

Figure 2.1. Verilog module for a full adder.

This module may be used as a building block for the hierarchical description of a more complex module, such as the four-bit ripple carry adder of Figure 2.2 whose Verilog description is shown in Figure 2.3. As before, the module description begins with a listing and then a declaration of all inputs and outputs. An interesting feature is in the definition of several vectors. For instance, the inputs p and q are defined as four-bit vectors, with bit 3 being the most significant bit; alternatively, if '[3:0]' were to be substituted by '[0:3]', then bit 0 would be the most significant bit. The next declaration of a `wire` corresponds, in this example, to an internal connection within the module. Finally, the description of the adder instantiates four copies of `full_adder` defined in Figure 2.1. Note that the order of the port connections corresponds exactly to the order used in the definition of `full_adder`[1].

Through the examples shown above, it is easy to see that the specification of the adder is very similar to writing a program in a high-level programming language. A Verilog compiler has the capability of translating this description to a hardware

---

[1] Verilog does indeed permit an out-of-order specification of the list of ports, but we prefer to avoid its use in this book.

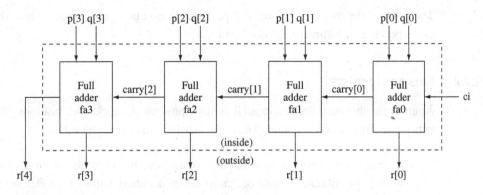

Figure 2.2. Schematic of a four-bit ripple-carry adder.

```
module RCA(p,q,ci,r);

input [3:0] p, q;        // Declaration of two four-bit inputs
input ci;                // and the one-bit input carry

output [4:0] r;          // Declaration of the five-bit outputs

wire [2:0] carry;        // Declaration of internal carry wires

full_adder fa0(p[0],q[0],ci,r[0],carry[0]);
full_adder fa1(p[1],q[1],carry[0],r[1],carry[1]);
full_adder fa2(p[2],q[2],carry[1],r[2],carry[2]);
full_adder fa3(p[3],q[3],carry[2],r[3],r[4]);

endmodule
```

Figure 2.3. Verilog module for a four-bit ripple-carry adder.

implementation to a specified target. This target could be a field programmable gate array (FPGA) implementation or a semicustom implementation using a standard cell library.

2.2 A more formal introduction to the basics

2.2.1 Modules and ports

As exemplified by the discussion in Section 2.1, a typical Verilog description is contained within a module, and this module may instantiate one or more copies of other modules. The body of each module contains a list of port declarations, followed by the description of the module, and terminated by the keyword endmodule.

The ports of the module may be of type `input`, `output`, or `inout`, where the last corresponds to a bidirectional connection.

2.2.2   Nets and registers

Apart from the port declarations, it is also possible to make declarations that are entirely internal to the module. These declarations may correspond to:

Net variables correspond to structural connections between two or more elements within the module. These are most often declared within a model using the keyword `wire`. Alternative specifications of nets also exist to define, for example, tristable nets (e.g., `triand`, `trior`), nets that can implement wired AND or wired OR logic functions (e.g., `wand`, `wor`), and power/ground nets (`supply1` and `supply0`). The default value of a `wire` data type is the tristate value **z**.

Register variables correspond to elements with memory that can store their value until they are next updated. The most commonly used register data type is denoted by the keyword `reg`, and its default value is the unknown value **x**. The differences between a register declaration and a hardware implementation of a register are subtle and include the fact that the former may or may not be clocked and may be changed asynchronously. In many cases, though, there is a one-to-one relationship between the two: the burden of ensuring this is placed on the designer, who can force synchronicity by updating the register variable in the Verilog description only on the onset of a clock.

Unless specified in terms of an array, both the `wire` and `reg` keywords represent a single bit. Particularly in the case of stored variables, more compact representations are often convenient. To facilitate this, Verilog permits register variables of type `integer` and `real` to store integer and real variables, respectively. For example, in specifying the value of a counter, an integer variable may be more convenient to use, and may make the description more readable than the use of an array of bits.

Another stored variable that is provided for convenience is the integer `time` data type, which is most commonly used in conjunction with the system function `$time` that provides the current time point of the simulation as an integer. A corresponding data type `realtime` can be used to store time in the form of a real number.

Verilog imposes stringent requirements on the mapping from the internals of a module to its ports, and these are summarized below. Since a port defines the connection to a module to the external world, it may be viewed from the inside of a module as well as from the outside. For the example of the full adder module that was used in a ripple-carry adder, the definition of the ports within module full_adder correspond to the view of that module from the inside. In module RCA, the data types of the ports in each of the four instantiations of full_adder correspond to its view from the outside. This is illustrated by the symbols 'inside' and 'outside' in Figure 2.2.

The following rules govern the mapping of ports of a module to nets or registers:

- From the inside, an input must be a net data type, but not a register data type. The connection external to the module may be either a register or a net.
- An output port may be either a net or a register variable from the inside, but must be a net variable on the outside.
- An inout port must be a net both from the inside and the outside.

The rationale for this convention could be understood by observing that the designer does not inadvertently specify a latency of more than one, i.e., two storage elements are not inadvertently connected in series. In cases where such a connection is desired, the notation permits such a connection through an explicit and conscious action of connecting a net to a register.

Note that the Verilog 2001 standard has a new feature that permits a statement of the form:

```
output reg a;
```

while in earlier versions of Verilog, this would have to be written as

```
output a;
reg a;
```

2.2.3   Vectors and arrays

It is often convenient to conceptualize groups of nets or registers in terms of an array, for example, in case of a bus or a hardware register. For this purpose, Verilog permits the definition of a vector for net and reg data types. For example, an eight-bit address bus may be specified using the declaration

```
wire [7:0] address;
```

where bit 7 corresponds to the most significant bit (MSB) and bit 0 to the least significant bit (LSB).

Examples of the use of this declaration were seen in Figure 2.3. It is interesting to note that it is possible to access an individual element of the vector, for example, by referring to address[2].

For the `reg`, `integer` and `time` data types, Verilog also permits the definition of an array. For example, the declaration

```
reg io_port[3:0];
```

corresponds to an array of four one-bit `reg` variables. Similarly, one may also declare an array of vectors such as

```
reg [7:0] cache[511:0];
```

which declares an *array* of 512 `reg` variables, each of which is an eight-bit wide *vector*[2].

A few common applications of vectors and arrays are:

- *Memory*, in the form of RAMs, ROMs or register files, may be modeled using arrays of vectors, as in the case of the cache declaration above.
- Strings of characters can be stored in `reg` vectors; the caveat here is that each character requires eight bits, so that a string of n bits requires the declaration of a `reg` vector of dimension $8 \times n$.

2.2.4 Constants

The keyword `parameter` in Verilog announces the declaration of a constant and assigns a value to it. Parameter values may be declared by providing their values with the description. For example, within a module `my_module`, one may define

```
parameter number_of_bits = 32;
```

The `defparam` statement in the upper level module permits the declared values of the parameter within a module to be overridden. For example, the value of the parameter `number_of_bits` in the module `my_module` may be overridden in the upper level module that instantiates it as follows

```
defparam x.number_of_bits = 16;
defparam y.number_of_bits = 64;

my_module x();
my_module y();
```

---

[2] It is important to observe that the above is a unidimensional array of eight-bit `reg` variables, and that Verilog does not permit multidimensional variable declarations.

The `my_module x();` and `my_module y();` statements will, respectively, instantiate the module `my_module` and override the value of the internally declared parameter, `number_of_bits`, from its default value of 32 to 16 and 64, respectively.

Alternatively, parameter instances can also be overridden during module instantiation. Consider a case where a module internally defines the following parameters

```
module xyz;
:
parameter p1 = 1;
parameter p2 = 2;
parameter p3 = 3;
parameter p4 = 4;
:
endmodule
```

When `xyz` is instantiated, the parameters may be overridden as follows

```
xyz #(5,6,7,8) xyz1;
```

This statement overrides the values of `p1` through `p4` with the numbers 5, 6, 7 and 8, respectively. Note that the order of parameters in the instantiation corresponds directly to the order in which they are defined in the module. If all of the parameters are not specified, then the parameters are overridden in order of appearance. For example, in

```
xyz #(11,12) xyz1;
```

the value of `p1` is set to 11, of `p2` to 12, and those of `p3` and `p4` remain at their default values of 3 and 4, respectively.

2.2.5   Number representation

Verilog permits numbers to be represented using a binary, octal, hex or decimal representation. Apart from the normally permissible values (0 and 1 for binary, 0 through 7 for octal, 0 through F for hex, and 0 through 9 for decimal), each digit may take on the values x (unknown) or z (high impedance).

A number may be represented in a *sized* or *unsized* form, depending on whether the number of bits is specified or not. A sized number is represented in the form

```
size ' base_format number
```

where `size` corresponds to the number of bits, `base_format` takes on one of the possible values of b (binary), o (octal), h (hex) or d (decimal), and `number` is the actual value of the number. It is important to note that regardless of the base that is used, the `size` refers to the number of binary bits in the representation. Examples of numbers in a sized format include

8'b11111111, 8'o377, 8'h FF and 8'd255

Note that, coincidentally, all of the above numbers represent the same value in different bases. It is worth reiterating that x and z are also permissible values for each digit in any base.

In contrast, unsized numbers are written without a size specification, which defaults to a value that varies with the simulator.

2.2.6   Operators

The statements within a Verilog description can be expressed in terms of a set of operations. Many of these may use the wide range of built-in operators that Verilog provides for the most commonly used operations; these operators are typically used to alter a set of operands on the right-hand side of an expression to generate a result that is assigned to the left-hand side.

The built-in operators in Verilog can be classified into several categories described below. Many of these operators are similar to those used in many other programming languages.

Arithmetic operators: These include the following that operate on two operands

Operator	Add	Subtract	Multiply	Divide	Modulus
Symbol	+	−	*	/	%

In addition, as in most other languages, + and − may act as unary operators on a single operand; for example −8 would negate the value of the number 8.

Logical, bitwise and reduction operators: These perform a set of basic Boolean or bitwise-Boolean operations, and are listed below. The Boolean operators perform logical operations on one-bit Boolean operands, yielding a Boolean result. In contrast, the bitwise-Boolean operators operate on binary words of multiple bits and perform bit-by-bit Boolean operations on the corresponding bits of each word. Reduction operators use the same operator symbols as bitwise-Boolean operators, but differ from them in that they operate on one operand instead of two, and yield a one-bit result. For example, the reduction AND of an eight-bit vector myvec, denoted as & myvec, is given by the logical AND of the eight bits of myvec.

Operator	Boolean			Bitwise-Boolean				
	and	or	not	and	or	not	xor	xnor
Symbol	&&	||	!	&	|	~	^	~^

Relational operators: Relational operators are used to verify the truth or falsehood of an expression, and return a Boolean value of 1 or 0, respectively, depending on the result. If no conclusion can be arrived at (for example, when there are x or z bits in the operands), then a value of x is returned.

A special case of this is the case equality operator, which returns either a 0 or a 1 in each case. If the operands contain x or z bits in the same positions, the result is a 1; otherwise it is a 0. As an example, if two variables A and B each hold the value xz1, then the '==' operator will return x, while the '===' operator will return 1.

Operator	greater than	less than	greater than or equal to	less than or equal to
Symbol	>	<	>=	<=

Operator	equal	not equal	equal (case)	not equal (case)
Symbol	==	!=	===	!===

Other miscellaneous operators: The shift operations perform a left (<<) or a right (>>) shift by a specified number of bits. To shift a reg variable A by four bits to the left, one simply writes the statement

```
A << 4;
```

These shifts correspond to logical shifts that shift zeros into the vacated bit positions.

Another useful operator performs concatenation of multiple operands and is a handy tool in hardware specification. A Verilog statement that concatenates variables X and Y and writes the result into Z is

```
Z = {X,Y};
```

It is worth pointing out that constant operands are also permitted for concatenation.

A special case of concatenation is the replication operator, which repeatedly concatenates the same number a specified number of times. To replicate the variable A twice and write it into B, one would simply write

```
B = { 2 {A} };
```

Finally, as in the C language, the conditional operator evaluates the truth of an expression and then performs either one operation or another, as follows:

```
condition ?: true_consequence : false_consequence;
```

These conditional statements may be nested, so that `true_consequence` may, for example, contain another conditional statement.

2.3   Behavioral and structural models

One of the advantages that many hardware description languages afford is in the representation of hardware at various levels of abstraction. In this section, we will consider the design of a simple finite state machine (FSM), and represent it at two levels of abstraction in Verilog:

Behavioral: At this level, the design is coarsely described at a high level of abstraction that resembles a high-level language, and the details of the precise implementation are hidden. An example of a behavioral description would be a program that describes the behavior of an FSM in terms of its state transition diagram.

Structural: This is considered to be a lower level of implementation, at which the design is finalized up to the gate or block level. For the FSM example, this could correspond to a selection of gates that implement the logic equations that relate the next state bits and outputs to the present state bits and inputs. Alternatively, the structural level could use blocks of greater complexity than a gate, such as an ALU, which could then be defined in a separate module.

Each level of abstraction is important during the design process. Design is an intrinsically hierarchical process in which the task of building a system is subdivided into multiple tasks of building subsystems that interact through a set of signals, and it is important to verify the correctness of the subsystems through the design process. Early in the process, the behavioral models for each block can be 'pasted' together through their interacting signals to ensure correctness. As we go further into the process, a more detailed model can be inserted to replace a more abstract model such as the behavioral model for one or more blocks in a system-level simulation. Moreover, each such detailed model for a block can be compared with its more abstract model for correctness, and this process lends itself towards a structured and disciplined design philosophy.

At higher levels of abstraction, the designer has a greater flexibility to change the system in a relatively painless manner. However, performance measurement at this level is relatively inaccurate since many of the system details are as yet undetermined. While this is resolved at the structural level, the design effort involved in making a significant change at this level is considerable.

A final point is that a typical design description may contain a combination of behavioral and structural descriptions.

2.3.1 An example of a finite state machine

We now present a specific example of a digital circuit that is described by Verilog at various levels of abstraction. We begin with an FSM description, and our example models the life of a typical medieval knight. As the knight sets off on a quest, he may first make preparations that involve polishing his armor, sharpening his sword, taking his horse to the vet for a checkup, etc. He would then seek a dragon to slay, and do battle until either the dragon or his courage were exhausted.

This may be modeled by a system whose inputs are

- the `adventure` signal, which indicates that the knight is seized with the spirit of adventure,
- the `sword_sharpened` signal, which is asserted when all preparations for the quest are complete,
- the `courage` signal, which measures whether the knight's valor is up to the task at hand, and
- the `dragon` signal, which indicates a live dragon nearby.

A state diagram that models this system is shown in Figure 2.4. We begin in state S0, where the knight remains until the `adventure` signal is asserted. At this point, a transition is made to state S1, where he prepares for his adventure. The signal `sword_sharpened` is set to true when these preparations are complete, and he sets off on his quest, to state S2. Even the bravest of knights could have an off day, and if his courage deserts him at this point (as signaled by the input `courage`), he returns to state S0. If, however, his courage remains strong, he remains in state S2 until a live dragon shows up. On the assertion of the signal `dragon`, a transition is made to state S3, where a battle with the dragon is fought in a single clock cycle. At the end of the clock cycle, if the dragon is vanquished, the signal `dragon` is asserted, and a transition is made to the final state S4, where the `quest_over` signal is asserted to show that the quest has been fulfilled. If, however, the dragon is still alive after the battle, the knight retreats to state S2, where he tests his courage reserves. If the

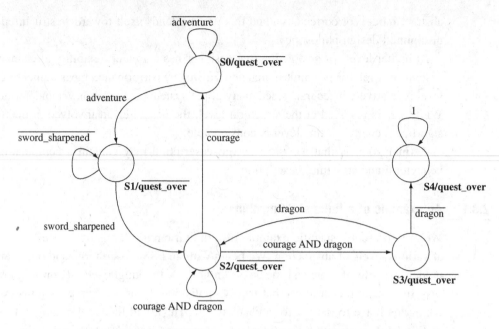

Figure 2.4. State machine for an FSM that models the life of a medieval knight.

dragon then flees, the signal `dragon` is asserted, and the knight remains in S2 until the next dragon appears, or until his courage fails him; otherwise, if the dragon stays to fight and the knight has ample reserves of courage, he returns to S3 for another battle with the dragon.

We will now write a Verilog description for this FSM, using various levels of abstraction.

2.3.2   Behavioral modeling

In this section, we will present a general guide to behavioral modeling using Verilog. The example of the medieval knight will be used to motivate an initial set of constructs, after which a broader set of constructs will be defined.

The Verilog behavioral model for the FSM is shown in Figure 2.5, in which the lines of code have been numbered for ease of explanation. The first observation that we make is that the description is essentially a translation of the state diagram in Figure 2.4 to Verilog code.

Studying the code segment that describes this FSM, we observe that the first set of 'define statements in lines 2–6 are used to set some parameters that are utilized within the program, similar to the #define statement in C. The parameters defined in these statements may be used within the rest of the description by prefixing the parameter by the ' symbol, as has been done on line 42, for example. Lines 8–17 provide the module definition, listing the inputs and outputs to the FSM, after

```
1.  // Definition of states
2.  'define S0  3'b000
3.  'define S1  3'b001
4.  'define S2  3'b010
5.  'define S3  3'b011
6.  'define S4  3'b100
7.
8.  module knight_life(adventure, courage, sword_sharpened,
9.                     dragon, clock, quest_over);
10.
11. input adventure;              // Declaration of inputs that
12. input courage;               // report on various
13. input sword_sharpened;       // aspects of a medieval
14. input dragon;                // knight's life
15. input clock;
16. output quest_over;           // (Set to 1 on completing quest)
17. reg quest_over;
18.
19. reg [2:0] present_state;     // Declaration of
20. reg [2:0] next_state;        // internal state variables
21.
22. initial
23. begin
24.   present_state = 'S0;
25.   next_state = 'S0;
26.   quest_over = 1'b0;
27. end
28.
29. always @(present_state)
30. begin
31.   casex (present_state)
32.     3'b0xx: quest_over = 1'b0;    // S0 through S3
33.     3'b100: quest_over = 1'b1;    // S4
34.     default: begin quest_over = 1'b0;
                     $display("Illegal state"); end
35.   endcase
36. end
37.
38. always @(present_state or adventure or courage
39.          or sword_sharpened or dragon)
40. begin
41.   case(present_state)
42.     'S0: if (adventure)
43.            next_state = 'S1;
44.         else
45.            next_state = 'S0;
```

Figure 2.5. Behavioral description of an FSM modeling the life of a medieval knight.

```
46.    'S1: if (sword_sharpened)
47.            next_state = 'S2;
48.        else
49.            next_state = 'S1;
50.    'S2: if (courage)
51.            if (dragon)
52.                next_state = 'S3;
53.            else
54.                next_state = 'S2;
55.        else
56.            next_state = 'S0;
57.    'S3: if (dragon)
58.            next_state = 'S2;
59.        else
60.            next_state = 'S4;
61.    'S4: next_state = 'S4;
62.    default: $display("Illegal state");
63.    endcase
64. end
65.
66. always @(posedge clock)          // Updates the state at
67.    present_state = next_state;    // positive clock edge
68.
69. endmodule
```

Figure 2.5. (Continued)

which internal state variables are described in lines 19– 20. Note that the output quest_over is also declared as a register to ensure that it holds its value.

The initial statement on lines 22–27 is a construct that we have not encountered as yet in our discussion. It is used to initialize the values of various internal and output variables at the beginning of the system simulation. A module may contain multiple initial statements, each of which is executed concurrently at time 0 of the simulation[3].

Line 29 introduces the always statement, which is performed repeatedly during the simulation. In this case, the always statement is qualified by the timing statement @present_state, implying that the statement is entered whenever the value of the variable present_state is modified during the simulation.

Lines 31–34 serve to set up the Moore outputs associated with the states 'S0, 'S1, 'S2, 'S3, and 'S4 using the casex statement. The case, casex and casez constructs are all very similar statements that are followed by an expression (we will shortly point out the differences between them). Depending on the value taken

---

[3] Be warned that not all simulators support the initial statement, and it is generally considered a nonsynthesizable construct, and may have to be set up during verification.

by that expression, one of the following alternatives is executed. For example, the value of `present_state` is tested on line 31 to determine which of the succeeding statements is to be executed. Line 32 corresponds to any state that has a zero in the first bit position, namely states 'S0 through 'S3, where `quest_over` is set to 0. When `present_state` corresponds to state 'S4, the statement on line 33 is executed to set `quest_over` to 1. The default statement corresponds to the case where none of the other alternatives is chosen, a situation that is not expected in our case. Nevertheless, it is considered good practice to insert, for example, a simple error statement for the default case, using the `$display` system call. Note that the output `quest_over` was listed as a `reg` variable on line 17; this is required since it is used to hold a value within a case statement. However, synthesizers will typically not assign a memory element to this `reg` variable, as long as it is assigned a value for all possible combinations of the case statement.

The difference between the various flavors of the case statements is simple: `case` requires all bit positions in the case alternatives to be precisely specified as either 0 or 1; `casez` permits bits in the case alternatives to take on the value z, and treats them as 'don't cares' in the comparison; `casex` permits x or z values and treats both as 'don't cares'.

Lines 38–64 use constructs that have been previously defined, and perform the function of setting the value of `next_state` whenever either an input or the `present_state` is altered, which triggers an entry into the `always` statement. The case statement considers the value of the inputs and encodes the transitions defined in the state diagram in Figure 2.4. We commend to the reader's attention the `if-else` construct, used for the first time on lines 42–45, which is rather self-explanatory.

Finally, lines 66–67 update the value of the state on the onset of the clock. The statement `always @(posedge clock)` indicates that this update is performed at the positive edge of the signal clock, thereby implying that positive edge-triggered flip-flops are used to construct the state machine. If negative edge-triggered flip-flops were to be used instead, the keyword `posedge` would have been replaced by `negedge`.

2.3.3   Other constructs for behavioral modeling

We now introduce several other constructs that are useful in behavioral modeling.

Timing controls

In the physical implementation of digital systems, various hardware components have nonzero delays. Verilog provides for statements that can model these delays at various levels of abstraction. The simplest delay assignment corresponds to an assignment statement, and is exemplified by the following statement:

```
# 10 a = b;
```

This assignment statement indicates that the program waits for 10 time units, after which a takes on the value of b, and for this reason, this type of delay is often referred to as a blocking delay. A different way of specifying the delay, which can end in different results, is the statement:

```
a = # 10 b;
```

The difference between this and the previous assignment statement lies in the fact that during simulation, it takes the value of b at the very time (in terms of the simulation clock) when the statement is encountered. It then sets a to take on that value 10 time units hence. This is unlike the earlier statement that samples the value of b only 10 units later. In other words, unlike the previous statement, which postponed the execution of the entire statement by 10 time units, this statement only postpones the assignment by 10 time units, and is equivalent to the statements:

```
c = b;
# 10 a = c;
```

where c is a temporary variable. Clearly, if b changes during these 10 time units, the result of the two assignments will be different.

   Timing controls in a Verilog description may also be inserted by the use of the @ keyword, as in lines 29, 38 and 66 of Figure 2.5. These correspond to the use of a signal edge for control. If, instead, level-sensitive control is desired, one may use the wait statement, which is of the type:

```
wait (signal_name)
begin
  (list of assignments)
end
```

Blocking and nonblocking assignments

An assignment statement is one that is used to update the value of a variable, and typically consists of a variable on the left-hand side and an equation on the right-hand side. We have encountered such statements frequently so far: as an example, consider line 24 in Figure 2.5. This assignment, which uses the = operator, is referred to as a *blocking* assignment. Blocking assignments that appear sequentially after each other within an initial or always block are executed sequentially during the simulation. For the code shown below, the first three statements are executed at time 0, the fourth at time 10, and the fifth at time 30, as shown in the comments.

```
initial
begin
  a = b;            // Executes at time 0 of the simulation
  c = 1'b0;         // Executes at time 0 of the simulation,
                    // but after a = b
  d = 1'b0;         // Executes at time 0 of the simulation,
                    // but after c = 1'b0
  #10 c = 1'b1;     // Executes at time 10 of the simulation
  d = #20 c;        // Executes at time 30 of the simulation
end
```

A subtle point here is that although the first three statements are executed at time zero, the order in which they are executed is strictly sequential. In other words, a = b; is first executed, after which c = 1'b0; is carried out, and then the assignment d = 1'b0; is completed, but as far as the simulation is concerned, all of these are said to execute at time 0. The importance of understanding the order in which the statements are executed is in realizing that a sequence of blocking assignments a = b; c = a; may not yield the same result as c = a; a = b;.

In contrast, the *nonblocking* assignment uses the <= symbol[4], and corresponds to a set of concurrent assignment statements, each of which can be considered to begin executing in parallel when the block of code is encountered during the simulation. The primary utility of nonblocking statements in Verilog is in modeling concurrent transfers in digital systems.

```
initial
begin
  a = b;            // Executes at time 0 of the simulation
  c = 1'b0;         // Executes at time 0 of the simulation
  d = 1'b0;         // Executes at time 0 of the simulation
  #10 c <= 1'b1;    // Executes at time 10 of the simulation
  d <= #20 c;       // Executes at time 20 of the simulation
end
```

If we consider the block of code shown above, it is superficially very similar to the previous example with blocking statements, with the difference that some of the = symbols have been replaced by a <= symbol. However, the result is entirely different from the case where blocking assignments are used. The first three assignments are

---

[4] Interestingly, this is also used to denote 'less than or equal to', and the meaning of the symbol is usually quite obvious from the context it is used in.

executed at time 0, the fourth at time 10, and the fifth assignment is now executed at time 20.

When a mixture of blocking and nonblocking assignments is used, the blocking assignments are first executed, followed by the nonblocking assignments. Consequently, in this example, d will take on the binary value 0 from time 0 to 20, and then switch to the waveform of c, delayed by 20 time units. Therefore, since c is at 0 until time 10, and then switches to 1, it follows that d will be at logic 0 from time 0 to 30, after which it changes to logic 1.

Loops

Like most programming languages, Verilog permits the use of loops for repetitive actions, with four types of constructs: forever, repeat, for, and while. These looping statements can only appear inside an initial or always block.

Forever loops are performed repeatedly throughout the simulation, once they are encountered. Perhaps the most common application is in generating a clock signal for simulation. An example that generates a clock signal of period 10 units is given by the code segment below:

```
initial
begin
  clock = 1'b0;
  forever
    #5 clock = ~clock;
end
```

Repeat loops execute a loop a fixed number of times. An example of a code segment that uses a repeat loop to initialize a register file is shown below:

```
parameter nbits = 16;
integer i;

initial
begin
  i = 1;
  repeat (nbits)
  begin
    regfile[i] = 0;
    i = i+1;
  end
end
```

For a good illustration of the use of a repeat loop, the reader is referred to page 135 of the IEEE 1364-2001 Verilog Standard, where a compact description of a multiplier implementation is provided.

For loops are very similar to those in C, and an illustration on the very same initialization example is shown below:

```
parameter nbits = 16;
integer i;

initial
begin
  for (i = 1; i <= nbits; i = i+1)
  begin
   regfile[i] = 0;
  end
end
```

While loops are executed as long as the condition associated with the loop is true at the entry point of the loop. The use of this loop for the the the same initialization step is shown below:

```
parameter nbits = 16;
integer i;

initial
begin
  i = 1;
  while (i <= nbits)
  begin
   regfile[i] = 0;
   i = i+1;
  end
end
```

2.3.4   Structural description

The behavioral level is a high level of abstraction that permits a description of the state diagram in Figure 2.4 in a manner similar to a high-level programming language. Taking the design one step closer to implementation involves the translation of the state diagram into a set of logic equations that relate the next state and the outputs to the present state and the inputs.

As in the behavioral description, we work with an encoding of the states, and as before, we will choose a simple scheme for encoding here, where the ith state Si is assigned using the binary number that corresponds to the integer i. However, the reader is reminded that the choice of state encoding can impact the circuit performance in several ways: firstly, depending on the binary assignments provided to the states, the amount of logic to be implemented can be different, particularly in a situation such as this where the 'don't care' space is large. Secondly, the average number of switching transitions, which translate directly to the power dissipation of the circuit, depends on the state assignment. A simple technique that is often used is to attempt to assign neighboring (in the Hamming distance sense) state codes to states that are connected by a transition edge, so that the number of switching state bits in each transition is minimized. Of course, this may not always be possible, and the task of the hardware synthesizer is to explore the design space for an optimal implementation.

For the state assignment that we have chosen, we can obtain, using routine techniques, a logic level implementation of the circuit in the form of the following Boolean equations

$$NS_2 = PS_2 + PS_1 PS_0 \texttt{dragon}' \tag{2.1}$$

$$NS_1 = PS_1' PS_0 \texttt{sword\_sharpened} + PS_1 PS_0' \texttt{courage} + PS_1 PS_0 \texttt{dragon} \tag{2.2}$$

$$NS_0 = PS_2' PS_1' PS_0' \texttt{adventure} + PS_1' PS_0 \texttt{sword\_sharpened}'$$

$$+PS_1 PS_0' \texttt{couragedragon} \tag{2.3}$$

$$\texttt{quest\_over} = PS_2 \tag{2.4}$$

where $NS_2 NS_1 NS_0$ and $PS_2 PS_1 PS_0$ correspond to the encodings for the next and present state, respectively.

The Verilog code describing this machine at a next lower level (sometimes referred to as the dataflow level) is shown in Figure 2.6. Unsurprisingly, lines 1 to 19, which deal with declarations and initializations, are substantially similar to lines 8 through 27 in Figure 2.5. One difference is that as we get closer to the hardware implementation, `next_state` is declared as a wire that updates a register holding `present_state`. In the succeeding lines 21 to 36, we encounter an assignment statement called a 'continuous assignment', denoted by the keyword `assign`[5]. This statement ensures that the value of the left-hand side is stored unless it is overwritten by the execution of another `assign` statement, or overruled by a `deassign` statement of the type `deassign variable_name;`. The `assign` statement can only be used for `reg` variables, and differs from the continuous assignment introduced in Section 2.3.2 in that the value for a register can be deassigned.

A useful attribute of the `assign` statement lies in its ability to model level-sensitive behavior. For example, it can be seen that if the inputs to this FSM change asynchronously with the clock, the `present_state` inputs will also change asynchronously.

At the next lower level of hardware description, the circuit describing the FSM can be mapped on to a specific set of gates. While the Boolean Eqs (2.1–2.4) describe the circuit at the logic level, they do not explicitly map the circuit on to gates.

---

[5] This was also encountered previously in the example in Figure 2.1.

```
1.  module knight_life(adventure, courage,
2.                     sword_sharpened, dragon, clock, quest_over);
3.
4.  input adventure;           // Declaration of inputs that
5.  input courage;             // report on various
6.  input sword_sharpened;     // aspects of a medieval
7.  input dragon;              // knight's life
8.  input clock;
9.  output quest_over;         // (Set to 1 on completing quest)
10. reg quest_over;
11.
12. reg [2:0] present_state;   // Declaration of
13. wire [2:0] next_state;     // internal state variables
14.
15. initial
16. begin
17.   present_state = 3'b000;
18.   quest_over = 1'b0;
19. end
20.
21. assign next_state[2] = present_state[2] || // equation (2.1)
22.   (present_state[1] && present_state[0] && ~dragon);
23. assign next_state[1] =        // equation (2.2)
24.                 (~present_state[1] &&
25.                   present_state[0] && sword_sharpened) ||
26.                 (present_state[1] &&
27.                   ~present_state[0] && courage) ||
28.                 (present_state[1] &&
29.                   present_state[0] && dragon);
30. assign next_state[0] =        // equation (2.3)
31.                 (~present_state[2] && ~present_state[1] &&
32.                   ~present_state[0] && adventure) ||
33.                 (~present_state[1] &&
34.                   present_state[0] && ~sword_sharpened) ||
35.                 (present_state[1] &&
36.                   ~present_state[0] && courage && dragon);
37.
38. always @(posedge clock)
39. begin
40.   present_state = next_state;
41.   quest_over = present_state[2];  // equation (2.4)
42. end
43. endmodule
```

Figure 2.6. Dataflow description of the knight's FSM.

For example, these expressions may be implemented in terms of a two-level sum of products, or as a multilevel logic circuit, and the choice made here can affect circuit performance parameters such as delay, area and power. While the description shown here is a gate-level structural description, it is also possible to show structural descriptions that use larger blocks such as MUXs or ALUs, which are separately defined in other Verilog modules.

A structural description of the FSM is described by the Verilog code in Figure 2.7. As before, the declarations and initializations remain essentially unchanged from the behavioral and dataflow code. The structural code utilizes a set of predefined gate types in Verilog. Each gate type is followed by an optional instance name (not used here) succeeded in parentheses by the output and the list of all inputs as follows:

```
out, in1, in2, in3, ...
```

(Of course, if the number of inputs is less than three, the list terminates with the last input.) The set of gate types includes the `and`, `nand`, `or`, `nor`, `xor`, `xnor`, `not` and `buf` (buffer) gates. Additionally, tristate buffers `bufif0` and `bufif1` are defined with the ordered parameter list

```
out,in,ctrl
```

For a `bufif0` buffer, the value of `in` is transferred to `out` when `ctrl` is 0; a `bufif1` is similar, except that the transfer occurs when `ctrl` is 1. The buffered inverters, `notif0` and `notif1` are similarly defined.

Lines 50 through 53 use instances of a module DFF that is defined separately in Figure 2.8.

Although the notion is not used here, it is possible to assign delays to the predefined gate types. If only one parameter is defined, it is used for all transitions: for example,

```
nor #(10) nor1(a1,a2,a3,a4)
```

is a three-input NOR gate with a delay of 10 units for all transitions. If two parameters are defined, they correspond to the rise and fall delay, respectively. For example,

```
nor #(3,4) nor2(a5,a6,a7)
```

is a two-input NOR gate with a rise delay of 3 units and a fall delay of 4 units.

2.4   Functions and tasks

In order to keep the Verilog code modular, functions and tasks are often invoked in writing a hardware description, and these play the same role as subprograms of various types in high-level languages. A function can have numerous inputs that are

```
1. module knight_life(adventure, courage,
2.                    sword_sharpened, dragon, clock, quest_over);
3.
4. input adventure;          // Declaration of inputs that
5. input courage;            // report on various
6. input sword_sharpened;    // aspects of a medieval
7. input dragon;             // knight's life
8. input clock;
9. output quest_over;        // (Set to 1 on completing quest)
10. reg quest_over;
11. wire questover;
12.
13. reg [2:0] present_state;  // Declaration of
14. wire [2:0] next_state;    // internal variables
15.
16. wire n1, n2, n3, n4, n5, n6, n7, n8, n9, n10, n11;
17. wire ps0_bar, ps1_bar, ps2_bar;
18. wire sword_sharpened_bar, dragon_bar;
19.
20. initial
21. begin
22.   present_state = 3'b000;
23. end
24.
25. not (ps2_bar, present_state[2]);
26. not (ps1_bar, present_state[1]);
27. not (ps0_bar, present_state[0]);
28. not (sword_sharpened_bar, sword_sharpened);
29. not (dragon_bar, dragon);
30. // equation (2.1)
31. and (n1, present_state[1], present_state[0], dragon_bar);
32. or (next_state[2], present_state[2], n1);
33. // equation (2.2)
34. and (n2, ps1_bar, present_state[0], sword_sharpened);
35. and (n3, ps0_bar, courage);
36. and (n4, present_state[0], dragon);
37. or (n5, n3, n4);
38. and (n6, present_state[1], n8);
39. or (next_state[1], n2, n6);
40. // equation (2.3)
41. and (n7, ps2_bar, ps0_bar, adventure);
42. and (n8, present_state[0], sword_sharpened_bar);
43. or (n9, n7, n8);
44. and (n10, ps1_bar, n9);
45. and (n11, present_state[1], ps0_bar, courage, dragon);
```

Figure 2.7. (Continued)

```
46. or (next_state[0], n10, n11);
47. // equation (2.4)
48. buf(questover, present_state[2]);
49.
50. DFF dff0(next_state[0], present_state[0], clock);
51. DFF dff1(next_state[1], present_state[1], clock);
52. DFF dff2(next_state[2], present_state[2], clock);
53. DFF dff3(questover, quest_over, clock);
54.
55. endmodule
```

Figure 2.7. Structural description of the knight's FSM.

```
module DFF(Q,D,clock);

    input D, clock;     // declaration of the list of inputs
    output Q;           // declaration of the list of outputs
    reg Q;

    always @(posedge clock)
    begin
       Q = D;
    end

endmodule
```

Figure 2.8. Verilog module representing a D flip-flop.

passed in as arguments to the function, but only one output that is returned as the value of the function. In contrast, a task may have a number of input, output or inout parameters that are returned through the arguments of the task. Other significant differences between functions and tasks lie in the fact that unlike tasks, functions always execute in zero simulation time and cannot contain delays. Moreover, while tasks can call other nested tasks or functions, this is not permissible for functions. We will provide examples of functions and tasks as we proceed further into this book.

2.5   Summary

This chapter has presented a quick, and not too dirty (we hope), introduction to Verilog, and could be considered an aid to help the reader get his or her feet wet. We reiterate that it is not intended to be a comprehensive introduction to the language, and we have primarily introduced the subset of constructs that will be most useful in following this book. As a consequence of this, there are several issues that have not been discussed, such as programming language interface, user-defined primitives and switch-level models. We will introduce subsets of these in the remainder of the book on an as-needed basis. In addition, we commend to the reader several good texts that deal more wholly with the Verilog hardware description language, such as those shown below.

Further reading

M. G. Arnold, *Verilog Digital Computer Design: Algorithms into Hardware*. Upper Saddle River, NJ: Prentice Hall, 1999.

J. Bhasker, *A Verilog HDL Primer*, 2nd edn. Allentown, PA: Star Galaxy Publishing, 1999.

M. D. Ciletti, *Modeling, Synthesis and Rapid Prototyping with the Verilog HDL*. Upper Saddle River, NJ: Prentice Hall, 1999.

IEEE Standard Verilog Hardware Description Language. IEEE Std 1364-2001, sponsored by the Design Automation Standards Committee, IEEE Computer Society, 2001.

P. R. Moorby and D. E. Thomas, *The Verilog Hardware Description Language*, 5th edn. Boston, MA: Kluwer Academic Publishers, 2002.

S. Palnitkar, *Verilog HDL: A Guide to Digital Design and Synthesis*. Mountain View, CA: SunSoft Press, 1996.

D. R. Smith and P. D. Franzon, *Verilog Styles for Synthesis of Digital Systems*. Upper Saddle River, NJ: Prentice Hall, 2000.

3 Defining the instruction set architecture

It's like building a bridge. Once the main lines of the structure are right, then the details miraculously fit. The problem is the overall design.

Freeman Dyson in Freeman Dyson: Mathematician, Physicist, and Writer,
Interview with Donald J. Albers, The College Mathematics Journal, 25, No. 1, January 1994.

Now that we have been introduced to the fundamentals of Verilog, we make a slight change in course to return to the top level of the design flow shown previously in Figure 1.2. In particular, we now discuss the process by which we define the instruction set of a new processor.

The *instruction set architecture* (ISA) of a processor defines all of the instructions available in the processor plus the storage elements that are accessible to the assembly language programmer. The contents of these storage elements, plus a few more that may not be directly accessible to the programmer, comprise the processor's *state*.

In this chapter, we show how the ISA of a complete processor, which we call the *Very Small Processor Architecture*, or VeSPA for short, is defined, refined, and ultimately specified. This processor is quite simple, with only slightly more than a dozen instructions. However, it is a complete processor capable of executing programs written in a high-level language compiled with an appropriate compiler. We use this processor throughout the remainder of this text as a vehicle for demonstrating the entire processor design process when using the Verilog hardware description language.

3.1 Instruction set design

The design of an instruction set for a new processor is more of an art than a science. The instruction set must be logically complete so that it is capable of executing any arbitrary sequence of operations that may be required by a program written in a high-level language. In fact, it has been shown that an instruction set with only one or two carefully chosen instructions can be logically complete. However, executing programs on such a processor is likely to be rather inefficient since even relatively simple operations could require complex sequences of the one or two instructions available in the instruction set. Furthermore, it may be difficult to implement what are likely to be rather complicated instructions in the hardware.

In developing a new instruction set, then, we want to ensure that we have enough different types of instructions available to allow the compiler to produce code that will efficiently execute the most common operations. We do not want to define too many instructions, though, since each instruction will be translated into some set of logic gates and registers that will ultimately be implemented in silicon. And this silicon will cost real money.

Our choice of specific instructions to include in the instruction set will involve numerous compromises and trade-offs. Our overall goal, however, should be to produce a processor that satisfies the following general criteria:

- It should be easy to write a compiler that can generate efficient code for the processor. Writing and verifying software to run on a processor is a very large component of the cost of any computer system. Consequently, to improve the productivity of the programmers, most programs are written in a high-level language. As a result, it is important that our instruction set is a good target for a compiler generating code for it.
- The processor should produce a level of performance sufficient for the given application. For a general-purpose processor, we may be interested in producing the highest level of performance possible. However, for an embedded system, such as the controller for a digital camera, or for some other low-cost application, we typically would want only the minimum level of performance necessary to meet the demands of the application.
- We must be able to produce sufficient quantities of the processor within our predefined cost constraints. Designing a processor with only the minimum level of performance needed by the application typically helps to minimize the cost. However, there are other design decisions we can make, such as the number and complexity of the individual instructions we choose to include, that also will have a direct impact on the cost of the processor.
- Finally, it should be relatively simple to build and verify. We could define complex instructions that satisfy the needs of the compiler, for instance. However, it may be very difficult to actually build a processor that implemented these instructions. More importantly, it may be hard to build a processor that includes these instructions and still satisfies the cost and performance constraints. It also could be very difficult to verify that the implementation is correct.

The choices made about the instruction set will significantly impact our ability to satisfy the above criteria. Experience has shown that, in general, instruction sets that are highly regular and include a relatively small number of instructions tend to have the best chance of allowing us to satisfy these criteria.

With these goals in mind, we can divide the various types of instructions we are likely to need in our processor into the following general categories:

- **Arithmetic operations**: The basic arithmetic operations are fundamental to the operation of any processor. Binary arithmetic operations take as inputs two *operand* values and produce a single output value. Addition, subtraction, multiplication, and division are all binary operations. Unary arithmetic operations, on the other hand, take a single input operand and produce a single result. Arithmetic negation, which is the same as subtracting a value from zero, is a unary operation commonly implemented in processors. Other unary operations include functions such as sine, cosine, and logarithms, for example.
- **Logical operations**: The logical operations manipulate the individual bits within values that are represented as binary numbers. The binary logical operations, that is, those that require two input operands, include AND, OR, and exclusive OR (XOR). The logical bit-by-bit complement operator, NOT, is an example of a unary logical operation.
- **Control operations**: Programmers assume that, unless directed otherwise, the instructions in a program will be executed in the order in which they appear in the source code. That is, they are executed in a straightforward sequential order. However, the real power of a computer system comes from its ability to compare values and make a decision based on this comparison. The decision typically reduces to a binary decision of either: 1) executing the next instruction in sequence if the comparison turns out FALSE; or 2) *branching* to a specified instruction somewhere else in the program if the comparison turns out to be TRUE. This type of operation is called a *conditional branch*. Other control operations include an *unconditional branch* in which the binary decision always evaluates to TRUE, and the similar *jump* operation in which the sequence of execution always transfers to the indicated target instruction.
- **Data transfer operations**: The data transfer operations are used to move values from one storage location to another *without changing the value in the source storage location*. Common data transfer operations are used to move values between registers or to read values from, or write values to, the memory. Note that these data transfer operations actually *copy* a value from one storage location to another instead of physically moving the value.

Each of these types of instructions must specify the operation itself, the operands on which it is to operate, and the next instruction to be executed. Since the most common next instruction to be executed immediately follows the currently executing instruction, it would be wasteful to have every instruction specify the next instruction in the sequence. Instead, we introduce the *program counter* (PC). The PC is a register that contains the address of the next instruction to be executed. It is automatically incremented by one instruction location as each instruction is executed. It thereby implicitly specifies the next instruction to be executed. With a PC, only branch and jump instructions need to explicitly specify the next instruction.

3.2   Defining the VeSPA instruction set

The first step in defining the instruction set for a new processor is to select the set of instructions from each of the above categories that will produce a logically complete set. Additionally, we want the instructions in this set to be simple to implement, and we typically want the smallest number of instructions necessary to efficiently execute the application programs. In the following sections, we describe the instructions we have chosen for the VeSPA instruction set as we discuss some important design decisions and trade-offs.

3.2.1   Arithmetic instructions

Determining which of all possible arithmetic instructions to include in the instruction set is typically the first step in which we are directly confronted with some important trade-offs. Not only do we need to determine which specific operations we would like to include, but we also need to determine how to specify the operands.

Specifying operands

As mentioned above, each of these instructions must specify the operation itself, the operands on which it is to operate, and the next instruction to be executed. We will assume that there is a PC to implicitly determine the next instruction to be executed. In specifying the operands, we can similarly specify them either explicitly or implicitly. If we specify each operand explicitly, each binary operation would need three fields, two fields to specify the input operands and one field for the destination operand. We can reduce the number of operand fields needed in each instruction, however, by implicitly specifying some of them. The number of operands we specify explicitly leads to the following options.

- **Three-address machine**: A three-address machine explicitly specifies both input operands and the destination for the output value in each arithmetic instruction. For example, the assembly language format for an add operation in this type of machine could be something like add r1,r2,r3 to specify that the sum of registers r2 and r3 should be placed in register r1. (It is common in assembly languages to have the destination register as the left-most register in the instruction. These semantics are meant to suggest those of a high-level language in which the left-hand side is the destination of an operation, such as r1 = r2 + r3.)

- **Two-address machine**: In a two-address machine, only the two source operands are specified explicitly. The destination operand is implicitly assumed to be the same as one of the source operands. For instance, add r2,r3 would place the sum of r2 and r3 into r2. This approach reduces the number of bits required in the instruction to specify operands. However, this reduction comes at the expense of less flexibility in specifying operands in the assembly language.
- **One-address machine**: A one-address machine specifies only a single source operand. The other source operand and the destination are implicitly assumed to be a special register, typically called the *accumulator*. The assembly language code add r2, for instance, would add the value in r2 to a special register called ac. The sum then is stored in ac. The one-address machine often is called an accumulator-based machine.
- **Zero-address machine**: The simplest form of an arithmetic instruction specifies only the operation to be performed while implicitly assuming the locations of both input operands and the result destination. This is precisely what happens in a *stack-based*, or zero-address machine. In this type of machine, the two input operands are assumed to be the top two elements of a special storage structure called the stack. An add instruction causes these two elements to be popped off the stack and added together with the result being pushed back on to the top of the stack. A stack is a very powerful data structure that is used frequently in various aspects of processor design. However, a stack-based machine is somewhat limited in the way it can access the necessary operands. As a result, stack-based machines are not particularly common. A notable exception, however, is the Java Virtual Machine (JVM) that is used to execute programs compiled from the Java programming language.

A three-address machine obviously will require more bits in each instruction to explicitly specify its operands compared to any of the other choices. However, a three-address machine may require fewer instructions to execute a series of operations from a high-level language than the other types of machines. In addition, arithmetic operations are most naturally expressed when explicitly specifying two operands and the destination. This feature tends to make the compiler writer's job easier than when writing a compiler for one of the choices that implicitly specifies one or more of the operands. Taking these various trade-offs into account, we have chosen to use the three-address format for the arithmetic operations in VeSPA.

Choosing specific instructions

We next need to determine the specific instructions to include in the instruction set. First, an ADD instruction is essential since add operations are performed very frequently in most programs. These ADDs are used not only for explicit arithmetic calculations, but they also are used extensively in most programming languages for address computations.

When using two's-complement arithmetic, a subtract instruction is not actually necessary since subtraction can be performed by adding the negation of the second operand to the first. That is, the operation $a = b - c$ is the same as the operation $a = b + (-c)$. However, negating the second operand requires at least one more instruction in addition to the add operation. Also, when comparing two values, it is convenient to have an explicit subtract operation in the instruction set. As a result, we have decided to include the SUB operation in VeSPA's instruction set.

For simplicity of implementation, we have decided not to include any additional arithmetic operations. Multiplications can be performed in VeSPA through repeated additions. While this approach is substantially slower than building a multiplier directly in hardware, it does simplify the design of the processor dramatically. Similarly, divisions would have to be performed using repeated subtraction, or some other division algorithm implemented as a sequence of the basic instructions available.

To summarize, we have defined VeSPA as a three-address machine with both an addition and a subtraction instruction.

Arithmetic overflow

One subtlety that arises in the arithmetic operations of a computer system is that, with a fixed number of bits available, there is a maximum absolute value that can be computed and stored. Trying to store a value larger than what will fit within the available number of bits will cause an *overflow*.

In a system that uses two's-complement arithmetic with n bits, one of these bits will be dedicated to the sign bit. This then leaves the remaining $n - 1$ bits to store the actual value. Thus, the largest values that can be stored are $\pm 2^{n-1} - 1$. Actually, the value -2^{n-1} is a legal value on many systems. However, for simplicity of explanation, we ignore this value in this discussion. See the references at the end of the chapter for more information about the trade-offs involved in representing negative values and two's-complement arithmetic. If the absolute value of a result produced by one of the arithmetic instructions is larger than $2^{n-1} - 1$, an error has occurred which must somehow be reported to higher level system software. The system may choose to ignore this overflow information. However, the processor designer still must ensure that overflows are detected.

To determine how to detect when an overflow has occurred, we can examine all possible combinations of signs of the two input operands and the result. In particular, if we add two values together that have opposite signs, it is impossible for the result to produce an overflow. If the two input values are both of the same sign, though, either positive or negative, it is possible for the result to overflow. What happens is that the sum will produce a carry-out from the most-significant bit of the absolute value of the result into its sign bit. Thus, when an overflow occurs, the sign bit of the result will be the opposite of the sign bits of the two input operands. All eight possible combinations are summarized in Table 3.1 showing which combinations indicate that

Table 3.1. *Determining the conditions under which two's-complement overflow can occur when computing* X + Y.

Input X	Input Y	X + Y	Overflow?
≥ 0	≥ 0	≥ 0	no
≥ 0	≥ 0	< 0	yes
≥ 0	< 0	≥ 0	no
≥ 0	< 0	< 0	no
< 0	≥ 0	≥ 0	no
< 0	≥ 0	< 0	no
< 0	< 0	≥ 0	yes
< 0	< 0	< 0	no

an overflow has occurred. A specific implementation for the corresponding overflow detection hardware based on this table is shown in Section 3.2.3.

Note that for subtraction, an overflow occurs when a borrow from the sign bit is necessary. Subtracting a negative value from a positive value must produce a positive result. Similarly, subtracting a positive value from a negative value must produce a negative result. If either of these conditions is violated, a borrow from the sign bit must have been performed indicating that a subtraction overflow has occurred. These requirements lead to the combinations shown in Table 3.2.

Arithmetic carry out

The above discussion concerned overflow of signed numbers computed using two's-complement arithmetic. The key consideration was a carry into the sign bit of the result during addition, or a borrow from the sign bit during subtraction. An analogous type of overflow can occur when computing with unsigned values. With n bits,

Table 3.2. *Determining the conditions under which two's-complement overflow can occur when computing* X − Y.

Input X	Input Y	X − Y	Overflow?
≥ 0	≥ 0	≥ 0	no
≥ 0	≥ 0	< 0	no
≥ 0	< 0	≥ 0	no
≥ 0	< 0	< 0	yes
< 0	≥ 0	≥ 0	yes
< 0	≥ 0	< 0	no
< 0	< 0	≥ 0	no
< 0	< 0	< 0	no

we can represent the unsigned values 0 to $2^n - 1$. Trying to compute a result that produces an unsigned value larger than $2^n - 1$ needs to be detected. This type of overflow is indicated simply by a carry out from the most significant bit. It often is useful to save this carry out bit in a special register to facilitate extended-precision arithmetic using special software routines. Saving this bit is addressed further in Section 3.2.3.

3.2.2 Logical operation instructions

The logical operation instructions, such as the Boolean AND, OR, exclusive-OR (XOR), and NOT, operate on the individual bits within a binary value. That is, there are no carries into or out of adjacent bits with these types of operations. For example, the logical AND of the binary values 1101 0011 and 0011 1011 produces the result 0001 0011. The Boolean NOT operation is a unary operation that simply complements each individual bit from the single input operand. The NOT of 1101 0011 produces 0010 1100, for instance. The NOT operation can be composed with the AND or the OR operations to produce the NAND and NOR operations.

In choosing which logical operations to include in a processor's instruction set, it is important to ensure that the selected set is *logically complete*. Logical completeness means that any of the basic logical operations can be computed using one or more of the operations available in the processor's instruction set. For example, DeMorgan's Theorem can be applied to compute the OR operation using only AND and NOT operations. Similarly, appropriate combinations of AND, OR, and NOT operations can be used to compute the XOR of any two values.

It can be shown that NAND by itself is logically complete, as is NOR by itself. However, computing an XOR using only NAND operations (or NOR operations) would require a relatively long sequence of instructions. We need to choose the logical operation instructions for our processor to balance the need for efficiency with the desire to minimize the number of instructions that we must implement. Given the frequent need for computing the various logical operations in many application programs, and the relative simplicity of implementing the basic operations, we decide to include the OR, AND, NOT, and XOR operations within VeSPA's instruction set. This combination allows us to compute the NAND and NOR operations using a sequence of only two instructions.

3.2.3 Control instructions

The control instructions alter the normal sequential execution of instructions that occurs with the steady incrementing of the PC. As mentioned previously, there are two basic types of control instructions: 1) the conditional branch, which alters the PC depending on the outcome of a test; and 2) an unconditional branch, or jump, that always alters the PC. The conditional branch must specify the operands to be tested, plus the condition for which the operands are being tested. In addition, both types of branches must specify the *target address* to which they will transfer control.

The target address is typically specified either as an absolute address to which the program should branch, or as an offset from the current value of the PC. The second form of specifying the target address is known as *PC-relative* addressing. The PC-relative approach allows every instruction to branch forwards or backwards the same amount from the branch instruction's location in memory. It also allows a program to be relocated in memory without having to recalculate all of the target addresses. However, it does require an adder to calculate the target address, *PC + offset*. The absolute addressing approach has the advantage of not requiring this address computation, plus the ability to jump directly to the desired address.

In VeSPA, we decide to implement the conditional branch instructions using PC-relative addressing to specify the branch target. The unconditional branch, which we will call a *jump* instruction, will use the absolute addressing mode for specifying the branch target. This approach of defining two types of control instructions is commonly used in the design of processors as it provides a good balance between the two methods of specifying the target address.

In addition to the desire to jump to an arbitrary address, high-level language features such as procedure calls and functions require the processor to implement some mechanism for jumping back to the instruction that follows the initial jump. To provide the basic operations necessary for this type of subroutine call and return, we include a variant of the jump instruction that saves the address of the instruction immediately following the jump into a designated register. We call this variant a *jump-and-link* instruction. The return operation is performed by jumping to the address stored in the designated *link register*.

The need to specify a condition to be tested, plus the operands to be used in the test, leads us to another trade-off in designing our instruction set. One approach is to incorporate both pieces of information (i.e., the condition and the operands) into the branch instruction itself. This leads to a set of *compare-and-branch* instructions. This approach has the advantage of specifying all of the information necessary to complete the branch in a single instruction. However, it is a relatively complex instruction in that it performs two essentially independent operations, the compare and the test of the condition, in one instruction. This complexity can lead to implementation difficulties which can end up impacting the processor's critical path delays and, thereby, the overall clock cycle time.

An alternative is to separate the compare from the test. With this approach, we end up with two different types of instructions. The *compare* instruction requires two input operands. Its output is one or more bits whose values are determined by the result of the comparison. The separate conditional branch instruction then tests the result of the compare instruction to decide whether or not to branch. Of course, some storage elements are needed to save the outcome of the compare until it is needed by the branch instruction. The outcome of the compare operation typically is stored in the processor's *condition code* bits. These bits are part of the processor's state. They are set by the *compare* instruction, and possibly by other instructions[1]. They are subsequently tested by the conditional branch instructions.

Due to the relative complexity of implementing a compare-and-branch instruction, we have chosen in VeSPA to use separate compare and branch instructions. The condition codes necessary to implement the various conditional tests are described next.

Condition codes

There are four condition code bits that are commonly set as a result of an operation or an explicit compare instruction. These specific conditions are chosen since a rich variety of conditional branches can be computed using these condition code bits. These bits are:

- **Carry bit – C:** The C bit is set to 1 to indicate that a carry out has occurred from the most significant bit of an unsigned operation. It is set to 0 if no carry occurs.
- **Zero bit – Z:** The Z bit is set to 1 if all of the bits in the result are 0. If at least a single bit is a 1, the Z bit is set to 0. Thus, this condition bit indicates that the arithmetic value of the result was zero.
- **Negative bit – N:** This bit is set to 1 when the result is negative. A 0 value indicates that the result was positive or zero.
- **Overflow bit – V:** The overflow bit is set to 1 if the result produces a two's-complement arithmetic overflow, as discussed in Section 3.2.1. The V bit is set to 0 when no overflow has occurred.

The logic required to calculate each of these bits is relatively straightforward. The carry bit (C) is simply the carry-out of the most significant bit of the ALU. Also, notice that, when using the two's-complement representation of values, a result is negative if the sign bit is 1. The N bit, then, is simply a copy of the most-significant bit of the result, which is the sign bit.

A logical OR of all of the bits in the result would produce a 1 if one or more of the bits in the result were 1. This is the complement of the definition of the zero bit

---

[1] Setting the condition codes is considered a side effect of instructions other than the compare instruction. This type of side effect can cause difficulties when trying to pipeline a processor. Consequently, it generally is a good idea to minimize the number of instructions that set the condition codes.

(Z). Thus, the Z bit can be calculated simply by forming the logical NOR of every bit in the result. Using Verilog's logical bit operators, we have

```
Z =~(| result[WIDTH-1:0])
```

where `result` is the output of an ALU with `WIDTH` bits. The vertical bar (|) is an operator that forms the bit-wise logical OR of every bit in `result`. The tilde (~) forms the logical complement (the NOT operator).

As we saw previously in Section 3.2.1, the conditions necessary for an overflow are slightly more complicated than those for determining the C, Z, and N bits. However, Table 3.1 really is a truth table showing when the overflow bit, V, is true. From this table we see that V should be 1 whenever the sign of the result is the opposite of the signs of the two input operands. These sign bits are simply the most significant bits of each of the three values. Continuing the example above using Verilog's logical bit operators, we have

```
V = (result[WIDTH-1] & ~op1[WIDTH-1] &~op2[WIDTH-1])
    | (~result[WIDTH-1] & op1[WIDTH-1] & op2[WIDTH-1])
```

The first term of this equation says that V is 1 if the result is a negative number but both operands are positive numbers. This is logically ORed with the second term which says that V is 1 if the result is a positive number but both operands are negative numbers. Thus, this equation says in Boolean logic exactly that an overflow occurs whenever the sign of the result is the opposite of the signs of the two input operands.

The above equation assumed that the operation being performed was an addition. Comparing Tables 3.1 and 3.2, we can see that determining whether an overflow has occurred for a subtraction operation is the same as for an addition operation, if we reverse the sign bit for the second operand before testing it in the above overflow equation. This observation leads to the following generalized equation for computing the V bit:

```
V = (result[WIDTH-1] & ~op1[WIDTH-1] & ~(subt^op2[WIDTH-1]))
    | (~result[WIDTH-1] & op1[WIDTH-1] & (subt^op2[WIDTH-1]))
```

In this equation, it is assumed that `subt` is an input to the logic that computes the condition codes. This input is set to 0 when the ALU operation being performed is an addition, and is set to 1 if the operation is a subtraction. The caret (^) in Verilog is the bit-wise exclusive-OR operation. Using this operator forces the sign bit of the second operand to be inverted when `subt` is 1.

Setting the condition codes

The compare instruction, CMP, is likely to be one of the most commonly used instructions to set the condition codes in VeSPA. This instruction is identical to the SUB instruction, except that it does not save the results of the subtraction. The only results it saves are the condition code bits. There are times when it is useful to actually save the results of the subtraction operation performed as part of a comparison, however, in addition to setting the condition codes bits. For instance, in a loop, it is common to subtract the loop stride value from the loop count variable and branch back to the top of the loop if the resulting value is not zero. By allowing the SUB instruction to set the condition code bits, we eliminate the need to perform an explicit compare operation to test the loop counter for zero. A similar argument can be made for allowing the ADD instruction to set the condition code bits. Thus, we decide to define the CMP, ADD, and SUB instructions in VeSPA as all setting the condition code bits.

In some processors, other instructions, such as the logical operations, also can set the condition code bits. This can be useful for testing the state of a particular bit or field of bits in a register. To minimize the number of instructions that have the side-effect of setting the condition codes bits, however, only the ADD, SUB, and CMP instructions set the condition code bits in VeSPA. As we shall see in Section 7.2, this decision will facilitate building a pipelined version of this processor by reducing the number of *hazards* between instructions.

Conditional branching

The whole point of defining the condition code bits is so that the processor can test them and make decisions based on their values. This is precisely the function of the conditional branch instructions. A typical use of these instructions would be first to compare two values using the CMP instruction. This comparison would do nothing more than set the condition code bits. One of the conditional branch operations then would read the appropriate condition code bits as inputs and branch or not, depending on whether the specific condition being tested evaluated to true or not.

Given that we have defined four condition code bits, it is logical to have four different conditional branches that check the value of each bit individually. Thus, we define the branch-on-carry-set (BCS), branch-on-overflow-set (BVS), branch-on-equal (BEQ), and branch-on-minus (BMI) instructions to branch if the corresponding condition code bit is set. Note that the BEQ is testing if the Z bit is set and that the BMI is testing if the N bit is set. Furthermore, the additional logic needed to test the complementary condition for each condition code bit is trivial, consisting of nothing more than a single inverter. This then leads to the branch-on-carry-clear (BCC), branch-on-overflow-clear (BVC), branch-on-not-equal (BNE), and branch-on-plus (BPL) conditional branch instructions.

While these branch conditions are quite useful, the power of the condition codes becomes apparent when we look at testing more complex relationships than simply whether a condition bit is set or reset. When comparing two signed values using the CMP instruction, the second operand is subtracted from the first operand. This comparison will produce a negative value if the first operand is less than the second operand. It would appear, then, that a branch-on-less-than (BLT) test should branch if the N bit is set after a subtraction using either the SUB or CMP instructions. However, if an overflow occurs as a result of the subtraction, the sign bit will be inverted from what it should have been if the first operand was actually less than the second operand[2]. In this case, the complement of the N flag should be tested. Thus, the condition to be tested for BLT is $(N \& \sim V) | (\sim N \& V)$. For the complementary condition, that is, branch-on-greater-then-or-equal-to (BGE), the test is simply the logical complement of this test, $\sim((N \& \sim V) | (\sim N \& V))$. After simplification, this test becomes $(\sim N \& \sim V) | (N \& V)$.

We can extend the BLT test to branch-on-less-than-or-equal-to (BLE) by noting that the Z bit will be set if the two operands are equal. The test for BLE then becomes $Z | ((N \& \sim V) | (\sim N \& V))$. The test for branch-on-greater-than (BGT) is the complement of this test which, after simplification, becomes $\sim Z \& ((\sim N \& \sim V) | (N \& V))$.

All of the branch conditions available in VeSPA, along with the corresponding tests of the condition codes, are summarized in Table 3.3. For completeness, we have included a branch-always (BRA) instruction and its complement, branch-never (BNV), in the instruction set.

Table 3.3. *The conditional branch instructions available in VeSPA, and the conditions they test.*

Conditional branch	Assembly	Condition code bits tested
Branch always	BRA	1
Branch never	BNV	0
Branch on carry clear	BCC	$\sim C$
Branch on carry set	BCS	C
Branch on overflow clear	BVC	$\sim V$
Branch on overflow set	BVS	V
Branch on equal	BEQ	Z
Branch on not equal	BNE	$\sim Z$
Branch on greater than or equal	BGE	$(\sim N \& \sim V) | (N \& V)$
Branch on less than	BLT	$(N \& \sim V) | (\sim N \& V)$
Branch on greater than	BGT	$\sim Z \& ((\sim N \& \sim V) | (N \& V))$
Branch on less than or equal	BLE	$Z | ((N \& \sim V) | (\sim N \& V))$
Branch on plus	BPL	$\sim N$
Branch on minus	BMI	N

[2] Notice that we allow overflows to occur in this situation so that we can compare two values that can both be represented within the number of bits available in the processor, even though their difference cannot be.

3.2.4   Data transfer instructions

In Section 3.2.1 we made the decision that VeSPA would be a three-address machine. That is, for the arithmetic and logical operations, VeSPA explicitly specifies in the instruction where both source operands are located, and the address of the destination where the result value is to be stored. What exactly do we mean by an 'address', though?

Load-store and memory-to-memory architectures

In the most general sense, an address is a number that tells the processor where to locate some storage element. From the processor's point-of-view, we typically have two basic types of addresses, a *register* address and a *memory* address. Registers are storage elements that are physically located near the processor in a *register file*. Consequently, they can be accessed very quickly, typically within a single clock cycle. The proximity of the register file to the processor and their high speed makes registers very expensive to implement, however. As a result, most processors have a relatively small number of registers available, typically on the order of 16 to 128.

A register address identifies a specific register within the register file. With a relatively small number of unique registers, only a few bits are needed for the register address. For instance, only six bits are needed to uniquely identify $2^6 = 64$ unique registers.

The main memory is a substantially less expensive array of storage elements (on a per bit basis) that also can be directly accessed by the processor. Due to the large number of memory locations, though, they must be located far away from the processor. This distance, combined with the type of technology that makes memories inexpensive, also makes them relatively slow to access. Furthermore, the memory address, which is a number that points to one particular word in memory, requires substantially more bits than the number of bits needed to address a register. Using 32 to 64 bits in a single address to specify one of 2^{32} or 2^{64} unique memory locations is common in today's processors, for instance.

In spite of the differences between registers and memory, they both can be used to store operands and results. The addresses used to specify the operands and the destination in the three-address VeSPA processor could be either memory addresses or register addresses. A *memory-to-memory* processor architecture explicitly specifies a memory address for each of the operands and the destination within the instruction. A *register-based* architecture, on the other hand, specifies the operands and destination using only register addresses. In this type of architecture, explicit load and store instructions are needed to move values between the registers and the memory. As a result, this type of architecture is commonly referred to as a *load-store* architecture.

There are numerous arguments about why one type of architecture is preferred over the other. It also is possible to mix the two approaches so that some of the operands are specified using register addresses while some are specified using memory addresses. Indeed, processors using a variety of approaches are produced today. However, one of the very nice features of a pure load-store architecture is that all of the instructions, except the load and store instructions themselves, need only a small number of register bits to specify the addresses of the operands and the destination. This characteristic allows all of the non-load/store instructions to fit into a common instruction format. This common format tends to simplify the design of the processor. In addition, explicitly identifying those instructions that access memory allows load-store architectures to perform certain types of optimizations that can hide the relatively long delay to access memory. Given these reasons, combined with the popularity of load-store architectures within the processor design community, we decide to make VeSPA a load-store architecture.

The VeSPA load-store instructions

We have defined three different load instructions and two different store instructions for VeSPA. The differences in these instructions are in the *addressing modes* they use to specify a particular location in memory. The load-immediate instruction (LDI) uses an *immediate* addressing mode in which the actual value to be loaded has been previously stored by the assembler within the instruction itself. Thus, the LDI instruction does not actually initiate a new memory access. Since the LDI instruction has already been fetched from memory, the LDI simply copies the value from the appropriate field in the instruction word and stores it in the designated destination register. This instruction is commonly used to initialize variables with constant values, for instance.

The load-direct (LD) instruction performs a basic read of a memory location and stores the value read into the designated destination register. This instruction uses a *direct* addressing mode in which the address of the desired location in memory is encoded directly into the instruction.

With the load-indexed (LDX) instruction, in contrast, a register address is encoded into the instruction as an operand, in addition to the address of the destination register. The contents of this source operand register are assumed to have been previously initialized with the address of the desired location in memory by other instructions executed by the program. This register is called an *index* register and the addressing mode is called *indexed* addressing.

We further extend this indexed addressing mode by allowing an *offset* value to be added to the contents of the index register. The offset value is stored as an immediate value within the instruction. The sum of the offset and the address in the index register then is the actual address in memory to be read. This *offset-plus-index* addressing mode is quite useful to compilers when generating the code needed to access parameters and local variables allocated on a run-time stack for procedure and function calls in high-level languages such as C.

We also define store instructions that correspond to the LD and LDX instructions. The store-direct (ST) instruction uses a direct addressing mode to specify the address of the location in memory to which the value in a specified source register should be written. Similarly, the store-indexed (STX) instruction specifies the destination address using the same offset-plus-index addressing mode as the LDX instruction.

In addition to moving values between registers and memory, it is convenient to be able to move values just between registers. Consequently, we define a special move (MOV) instruction that copies the contents of one register into another register. We do not actually implement this instruction in hardware, however. Instead, the assembler automatically converts this instruction into an ADD instruction where the second operand is the value 0. Adding zero to the contents of a register and storing the result is equivalent to copying the contents of the source operand register into the destination register.

The MOV instruction is an example of a *pseudo-instruction*. That is, it exists only in the assembler, although it can be used by an assembly language programmer as if it were actually implemented in the hardware. Notice that this instruction has the side-effect of setting the condition code bits since it is converted into an ADD instruction.

3.2.5   Miscellaneous instructions

Perhaps somewhat surprisingly, it is often useful to have an instruction that does no work. For example, if we wish to insert a fixed delay into a program, we could put this instruction into a loop and execute it as many times as necessary to obtain the desired delay. It also may useful to have this type of instruction in some pipelined implementations of the processor, as discussed in Section 6.3.2.

We could implement this type of *no-operation*, or *no-op*, instruction using some appropriate combination of existing instructions. For example, moving a register to itself with the MOV instruction is effectively a no-op. However, we must be careful about any side effects caused by the instruction. In the case of the MOV, for instance, the condition codes would be affected. The cleanest approach is to define a special instruction, which we will call NOP, that does no work and has no operands, outputs, or side effects.

Finally, it is useful to have an instruction to indicate that the processor should terminate its processing. In VeSPA we define the *halt* instruction (HLT) to stop the processor from fetching and executing any more instructions. Note, though, that in most systems there will be an operating system that runs continuously. Consequently, in many situations the HLT instruction is unnecessary. However, we will find the HLT instruction to be useful in terminating a Verilog simulation.

3.3 Specifying the VeSPA ISA

In the previous section, we determined the set of instructions we want to include in our processor. Before we can begin to build simulation models for this processor, however, we need to very carefully specify exactly what each instruction does and the ways in which they affect the storage elements that comprise the processor's state. This *instruction set architecture* (ISA) specification precisely defines for the assembly language programmer and the compiler writer what each instruction does, what registers it changes, what inputs it expects, and so forth.

You can think of this ISA specification as a detailed contract between the processor architect and the programmers. It also provides a contract between the architect and the logic designers who ultimately will implement this ISA in actual hardware. As long as both the programmers and the logic designers satisfy the conditions specified in this ISA 'contract', the architect is guaranteeing that their programs will run as expected on any processor that is designed to this ISA specification.

At this stage we do not want to specify how each instruction accomplishes its operations, though. We want to leave the details of the implementation to lower levels of the design hierarchy. This approach allows us to define a single ISA that can have many different underlying implementations. These different implementations may be designed to satisfy different cost and performance constraints, for instance. However, by maintaining the same ISA across several different implementations, we maintain the ability to run the same binary object file produced by the assembler (or directly by the compiler) on the different implementations. The performance of each implementation may be different, but, by making sure each implementation adheres to the ISA specification, we are assured that the programs will run correctly.

3.3.1 The instruction format

We are now at the point where we have to make some firm decisions about certain features of the processor, such as the number of registers and the basic word size. As we make these decisions, we will continue to be confronted with trade-offs and we will close off certain options. Nevertheless, we must decide on specific values for these features to allow us to specify the *instruction format*. This format determines how each of the bits in an instruction will be interpreted by the processor when it is fetched from memory and executed.

We begin by somewhat arbitrarily deciding that this will be a 32-bit machine. That is, each register will be capable of holding a 32-bit value. This decision also implies that the ALU and data paths likely should be 32-bits wide as well. For consistency, we decide that memory addresses will be 32-bits, and that the memory should be byte-addressable. That is, each 32-bit memory address points to a unique eight-bit location in the memory. Finally, we again arbitrarily decide that VeSPA will have 32 registers in its register file. We could have chosen more or fewer, but 32 seems like a reasonable balance between a sufficiently large number of registers and the number of bits required to address these registers.

Given that we have defined the memory to be byte-addressable, it would seem reasonable to define the instruction format such that each instruction fits in some whole number multiple of eight bits. Experience has shown that the implementation tends to be simpler if all of the instructions in a processor have the same number of bits. That is, it is convenient for all of the instructions to have a fixed length. This fixed length will simplify the fetching and decoding of each instruction. Since we have a 32-bit basic architecture, it seems reasonable that we should make all of the instructions fit into four bytes to make a 32-bit instruction word.

To define the instruction format, we must determine how the 32 bits for each instruction are partitioned into appropriate *fields* (groups) of bits. These fields are used to represent the operation to be performed, the source operand register numbers, the destination register number, the target address of a conditional branch, the condition to be tested, and so on. As much as possible, these fields should be aligned among the different instruction types. That is, if we decide that bits 22–26 should be the field to identify the first operand for the ADD instruction, we want to make sure that these same bits are used for the first operand field in all of the instructions. This type of alignment will significantly simplify the hardware required to decode the fields compared to a processor in which the fields are defined differently for each instruction.

Looking over the instructions that we have defined for VeSPA in the previous section, we find 14 arithmetic, logical, and miscellaneous operations (including CMP), two different types of jump instructions, and 14 different conditional branches. It would appear, then, that we need five *opcode* bits to uniquely specify each operation available in the instruction set since five bits provides $2^5 = 32$ unique bit patterns. However, it we think a little more deeply about branch instructions, for instance, we notice that they all perform exactly the same operation. The only difference among them is the condition that they test. So, instead of having separate opcodes for each of the conditional branches, we decide to devote a single opcode, which we call Bxx, to the conditional branches. We will use another field within this conditional branch instruction to distinguish among the different conditions being tested.

Similarly, the JMP and JMPL instructions perform almost identical operations. The only difference is that JMPL also stores the return address value in the specified link register. Consequently, we will dedicate one opcode for the JMP and JMPL instructions with an additional bit used to specify whether the return address should be saved or not.

After these consolidations, we find that we have only 16 unique instructions. These can be distinguished using a four-bit opcode field. However, to give us room to grow in the future by adding new instructions, we decide to allocate five bits to the opcode field, as shown in Figure 3.1. These opcode bits are absolutely fixed for every instruction in VeSPA. The processor needs to decode only these five bits to determine the instruction it is executing. We arbitrarily assign opcode values to the instructions as shown in Table 3.4. In the next section, we define the remainder of the instruction format for the individual instructions as we describe their detailed operation.

31 · · · 27	26 · · · 0
CCCCC	xxx xxxx xxxx xxxx xxxx xxxx xxxx
opcode bits	operand specifiers, etc.

Figure 3.1. The basic instruction format of the VeSPA processor showing the location of the opcode field.

Table 3.4. *The operations and corresponding opcodes defined for the VeSPA processor.*

Mnemonic	Opcode Decimal	Opcode Binary	Operation
NOP	0	00000	No operation.
ADD*	1	00001	Addition.
SUB*	2	00010	Subtraction.
OR	3	00011	Bit-wise logical OR.
AND	4	00100	Bit-wise logical AND.
NOT	5	00101	Bit-wise logical complement.
XOR	6	00110	Bit-wise logical exclusive OR.
CMP*	7	00111	Arithmetic comparison.
Bxx[†]	8	01000	Conditional branch (xx = specific condition).
JMP	9	01001	Jump indirectly through a register + offset.
JMPL	9	01001	Jump and link indirectly through a register + offset.
LD	10	01010	Load direct from memory.
LDI	11	01011	Load an immediate value.
LDX	12	01100	Load indirect through index register + offset.
ST	13	01101	Store direct to memory.
STX	14	01110	Store indirect through index register + offset.
HLT	31	11111	Halt execution.
Assembler pseudo-instructions.			
MOV*			Move (actually copy) one register to another.

* These instructions set the condition code bits.
[†] This instruction reads the condition code bits.

3.3.2 Instruction specifications

Now that we have determined the basic instruction format, the number of registers, the number of address bits, and so on, we can precisely define the operation of each instruction. A complete assembly language programmer's guide to these instruction definitions is given in Appendix A. In the following, we describe the reasoning behind the choices made in this ISA.

Arithmetic and logical instructions

Each of the arithmetic and logical instructions, including ADD, AND, XOR, OR, and SUB, must specify two source operand registers and a destination register in addition to the opcode. Since we have 32 registers, five bits will be needed to specify each operand and the destination for a total of 15 bits. Including the five opcode bits, 20 bits will be needed to completely specify these instructions, which easily fits within the 32 bits available.

However, this encoding leaves 12 bits unused in each of these instructions. It seems unfortunate to waste all of these undefined bits. In fact, we can take advantage of these available bits by slightly altering the definition of one of the source operands. Instead of requiring both operands to always be in registers, we can allow one of the operands to be specified using an immediate addressing mode. In this mode, the actual value of the operand, instead of its address, can be encoded into the extra bits available in these instructions. Note that we will need one of these bits to indicate the addressing mode for this operand, that is, whether the corresponding instruction bits should be interpreted as a register number or as an immediate value.

This extension to allow two different addressing modes for one of the source operands leads to the instruction encoding shown in Figure 3.2. We have chosen the bits immediately following the opcode, bits 26–22, to represent the destination register number, rdst. The next five bits, 21–17, specify the register containing one of the operands, rs1. The next bit, however, bit 16, is used as a mode bit to indicate which addressing mode is being used for the second operand. If this bit is a 0, then bits 15 to 11 should be interpreted as the address of a register that contains the second operand, rs2. However, if this bit is a 1, then bits 15 to 0 should be interpreted as the actual value to be used for the second operand.

31 ··· 27	26 ··· 22	21 ··· 17	16	15 ··· 11	10 ··· 0
opcode	rdst	rs1	0	rs2	00 0000 0000

31 ··· 27	26 ··· 22	21 ··· 17	16	15 ··· 0
opcode	rdst	rs1	1	immed16

Figure 3.2. The instruction format for the arithmetic and logical operations.

Note that there is a slight wrinkle in interpreting this immediate field. Only 16 bits are available to store this value. However, our processor operates on 32-bit quantities. Somehow this 16-bit field must be extended to a 32-bit quantity. Yet again, we have a choice to make. One choice is to treat this 16-bit field as an unsigned integer. In this case, we simply insert zeros into the most-significant 16 bits to make it a 32-bit value. The other choice is to treat it as a signed integer. In this case, we must *sign-extend* the value to convert it from a 16-bit value to a 32-bit value. Sign extension is done simply be filling the most significant bits with copies of the sign bit, which is bit 15 in this case. Either choice would be 'correct'. In the case of VeSPA, we decide to treat this immediate operand as a signed integer, and so specify that this immediate field will be sign-extended before the operation takes place. This immediate field thus can contain a value in the range $\pm 2^{15} - 1$.

The requirements for specifying the CMP instruction are almost identical to these instructions. The only difference is that CMP does not need to specify a destination register. Thus, we use the same instruction format for CMP, except that the destination register field will be ignored by the processor. It is conventional (and good engineering practice) to specify that these unused bits should be all zero.

Similarly, the requirements of the NOT instruction are almost the same as the other instructions in this category. The difference in this case, however, is that NOT needs to specify only a single source operand. Thus, the format for this instruction is specified to be the same as the other instructions in this category, except that the `rs2` field should be ignored by the processor when the instruction is executed. We also do not allow the immediate addressing option with this instruction since the NOT of any constant value could be calculated by the compiler or assembler. An LDI instruction then would be the best choice to use to load this constant value instead of using a NOT instruction.

Control instructions

In addition to the standard opcode field, the conditional branch instruction needs to specify the condition to be checked and the address to which the program should branch if the condition is true. If the condition evaluates to false, the program continues executing with the instruction immediately following the branch.

Specifying the branch condition in the instruction format is quite straightforward. Table 3.3 listed the 14 conditions that we can test with the conditional branch instruction. We encode which condition is being tested in the `cond` field in bits 26 to 23 shown in Figure 3.3. The specific encodings assigned to each condition test are shown in Appendix A.

When specifying the branch target address, we are again confronted with several options and trade-offs. As stated previously, we very much want to maintain a fixed-size instruction format. Thus, as shown in Figure 3.3, we have bits 22 to 0

31 $\cdots$ 27	26 $\cdots$ 23	22 $\cdots$ 0
01000	cond	immed23

Figure 3.3. The instruction format for the conditional branch instruction.

available to encode the branch target address. Furthermore, for performance considerations, we would like the branch target address to be fully encoded in this 23-bit field. Since branches are quite common, we do not want to have to load the target address into one of the registers before each branch instruction, for instance. Unfortunately, we cannot fully encode a complete 32-bit memory address into the 23-bit field available in the instruction. The trade-off we decide to make is to encode only 23 bits of the 32-bit branch target address into the conditional branch instruction.

Having made this decision, our next choice is how to interpret this 23-bit value. One option is to interpret it as an absolute memory address. This implicitly requires us to fill in the nine missing high-order bits with 0. The problem with this option is that branches can only branch to instructions within the address range 0 through $(2^{23} - 1)$. That is, with this approach, it is impossible to specify a branch target address larger than 2^{23}. This is a very severe restriction on the processor, and one that actually is unnecessary.

An alternative approach, and the one we choose for VeSPA, is to interpret this 23-bit immediate field as an offset value from the current PC value. That is, the branch target address is determined by adding the sign-extended value stored in this immediate field to the current value of the PC. This allows the conditional branch instructions to branch forwards or backwards to any address within $\pm 2^{22} - 1$ addresses of the branch instruction itself.

Actually, there is one small peculiarity that we must take into account with this addressing mode. While the branch instruction is being executed, the PC has already been incremented to point to the next instruction following the branch. Since each instruction is four bytes, and the addresses in VeSPA point to a byte in memory, the value of the PC is actually four larger than the address of the branch instruction itself. Thus, the value stored in this immediate field should be

(the address of the branch instruction) $-$ (the address of the branch target) $- 4$.

While this *PC-relative* addressing approach does not allow us to access the entire memory space with a single conditional branch, it does provide an attractive compromise among all of our conflicting requirements.

In contrast to the conditional branch instructions, which are constrained to branching within a limited range forwards or backwards from the instruction's address, we would like the jump instructions to be able to directly jump to any location in the address space. This requirement means that 32 bits are needed to specify the jump target address. Since five bits of the instruction are dedicated to the opcode, the only way to specify a complete 32-bit target address while keeping the instruction size fixed at 32 bits is by storing the target address in a register. Thus, the JMP and JMPL instructions specify the jump target address by encoding a register address into the instruction. This register must have been initialized with the desired jump target address by instructions executed before the jump instruction.

The JMP instruction needs to specify only a single operand – the address to which it is to jump. So, its encoding requires only the address of the register that contains the target address. The JMPL also needs to specify this jump address plus a destination register in which to store the return address. We also need a bit to indicate whether this is a JMP or a JMPL operation. These various requirements lead to the instruction encoding shown in Figure 3.4 for the two flavors of the jump instruction.

As always, bits 31 to 27 are reserved for the opcode. The `rs1` field in bits 21 to 17 specifies the register containing the jump target address. If bit 16, which we call the *link* bit, is 1, bits 26 to 22 are interpreted as the `rdst` field, which is the register number in which to store the return address, that is, the value currently in the PC. If this link bit is a 0, this field is ignored and no return address is saved.

At this point, we could ignore bits 15 to 0 and say that the jump instruction has been completely defined. However, we extend the functionality of this instruction by defining these extra bits to be a signed immediate field. This immediate value is sign-extended and added to the address stored in register `rs1` to form the actual jump target address. Typically this immediate field would be set to zero so that the jump will be directly to the address in `rs1`. However, this type of *jump-with-offset* operation can be useful when implementing jump tables in software, for instance. We have decided to include this feature in the jump instruction since it costs very little to add it.

Data transfer instructions

The load-immediate (LDI) instruction must specify the opcode, the immediate value to be stored, and the destination register into which the value is to be stored. Since five bits are needed for the opcode and another five bits are needed to specify the destination register, 22 bits remain for the immediate value, as shown in Figure 3.5. Interpreting this value as a signed two's-complement integer allows the LDI instruction to load values in the range $\pm 2^{21} - 1$.

JMP	31 $\cdots$ 27	26 $\cdots$ 22	21 $\cdots$ 17	16	15 $\cdots$ 0
	01001	00000	rs1	0	immed16
JMPL	31 $\cdots$ 27	26 $\cdots$ 22	21 $\cdots$ 17	16	15 $\cdots$ 0
	01001	rdst	rs1	1	immed16

Figure 3.4. The instruction format for the two jump instructions.

31 ··· 27	26 ··· 22	21 ··· 0
opcode	rdst	immed22

Figure 3.5. The instruction format for the LDI and LD instructions.

The format for the load-direct (LD) instruction is identical to that of the LDI instruction. The only difference is that for the LD, the value in the immediate field is interpreted as an address that contains the value to be read, instead of the value itself. Notice that this interpretation limits the range of addresses that can be accessed by the LD instruction. In particular, since this field is only 22 bits, the LD can access only 2^{22} unique locations out of the 2^{32} available in the address space. Furthermore, we decide to interpret this address using sign extension. Positive values then will translate into addresses in the range 00 0000 – 1F FFFF while negative values will be interpreted as addresses in the range FFE0 0000 – FFFF FFFF.

The format for the load-indexed (LDX) instruction is similar to the LDI and LD instructions. The difference is that we must use five bits from the immediate field to specify the index register. This leads to the format shown in Figure 3.6, where the `rs1` field specifies the index register.

The format for the store-direct instruction (ST) is the same as that for the LD instruction, except that the `rdst` field in bits 26 to 22 of the LD instruction is now interpreted as the number of the source register. That is, in the format shown in Figure 3.7 for the ST instruction, the substituted `rst` field is the address of the register whose value is to be written to memory at the address specified by the immediate field in bits 21 to 0. As in the LD instruction, the immediate value is sign-extended so that it accesses the same range of addresses as the LD.

The format for the store-indexed (STX), shown in Figure 3.8, is chosen to follow the format of the LDX instruction as closely as possible. However, as with the ST instruction, the `rst` field in bits 26 to 22 is interpreted as the source operand register.

31 ··· 27	26 ··· 22	21 ··· 17	16 ··· 0
01100	rdst	rs1	immed17

Figure 3.6. The instruction format for the LDX instruction.

31 ··· 27	26 ··· 22	21 ··· 0
01101	rst	immed22

Figure 3.7. The instruction format for the ST instruction.

31 ⋯ 27	26 ⋯ 22	21 ⋯ 17	16 ⋯ 0
01110	rst	rs1	immed17

Figure 3.8. The instruction format for the STX instruction.

Recall that the MOV instruction is a pseudo-instruction that gets converted into an ADD by the assembler. Therefore, the encoding of the MOV instruction will be the same as the ADD.

Miscellaneous instructions

Both the HLT and NOP instructions require no operands to be specified. The instruction encodings for these two instructions require only the opcode field. The remaining bits can be any value since they will be ignored by the processor. However, it is conventional to set all unused bits to zero.

3.4 Summary

The instruction set architecture (ISA) of a processor precisely defines the interface between the hardware designers and the software developers. In this chapter, we demonstrated with the example VeSPA processor the steps a computer architect would use to develop the ISA for a new processor. We discussed several of the important design trade-offs that face the architect, such as the various approaches to specifying an instruction's operands and how to go about choosing specific instructions to include in the ISA. We also showed how condition codes can be calculated and used to create a rich variety of conditional branch instructions. Finally, we defined the instruction format for each instruction in VeSPA and precisely specified how each instruction operates.

The next step is to build a behavioral simulation model to experiment with this new processor specification. This model will allow us to validate that our specification is complete and that our trade-offs were appropriate. If it turns out we made some poor trade-offs, or we need to more precisely specify certain operations, we can always return and change the ISA specification, at least until we release the specification to the programmers.

Further reading

The following texts discuss in greater depth the trade-offs involved in designing a processor's instruction set. They also describe several other instruction set architectures that have been implemented in different processors.

V. C. Hamacher, Z. G. Vranesic, and S. G. Zaky, *Computer Organization. 4th edn.* McGraw-Hill, 1996. *See Chapters 2 and 8 in particular.*

V. P. Heuring and H. F. Jordan, *Computer Systems Design and Architecture.* Addison-Wesley, 1997. *See Chapter 2 and 3 in particular.*

D. A. Patterson and J. L. Hennessy, *Computer Organization and Design: The Hardware/Software Interface.* Morgan Kaufmann Publishers, 1998. *See Chapter 3 in particular.*

B. Wilkinson, *Computer Architecture: Design and Performance.* Prentice Hall, 1996. *See Chapter 2 in particular.*

4 Algorithmic behavioral modeling

> The sciences do not try to explain, they hardly even try to interpret, they mainly make models. By a model is meant a mathematical construct which, with the addition of certain verbal interpretations, describes observed phenomena. The justification of such a mathematical construct is solely and precisely that it is expected to work.
>
> *John Von Neumann*

In the previous chapter, we defined the instruction set architecture for the VeSPA processor. This ISA definition includes all of the storage elements that comprise the processor's state and are accessible to the assembly language programmer. It also includes a description of each instruction and how it affects these state elements. Our next step is to develop a simulation model of this ISA to verify that our instruction definitions are complete, that we have included the right mix of instructions, that the state elements we defined are appropriate, and so forth. Our completed simulation model will be capable of executing programs written in the processor's machine language. (In the next chapter, we describe an assembler for generating machine language programs.)

Our goal in this chapter is to develop an *algorithmic behavioral* model of the VeSPA processor. This type of model describes what each instruction does while ignoring the implementation details needed to actually construct the logic that ultimately will produce this behavior. For example, at this stage, we do not care whether the ALU uses a ripple-carry adder or a carry-lookahead adder. We are concerned only that the ADD instruction causes the sum of two values stored in the register file to be written to the correct destination register. One important consideration is that this behavioral model ignores all timing information. The specific timing of the individual operations is left to the lower level models.

We describe the processor in an algorithmic fashion using the C language-like syntax and features of Verilog. This behavioral model does not make use of the full power and complete features of the Verilog language, though. Instead, we describe only those features and language constructs that are needed to write this behavioral model. The appropriate features are introduced as they are needed. If we have defined the ISA completely, we should find that developing this behavioral model reduces to almost a direct translation of the ISA definition in Appendix A into the corresponding Verilog equivalent.

```
module vespa;
// Declare global parameters
// Declare storage elements in ISA
// Declare internal registers for ALU operations
// Define opcode and condition codes
// Define fields in instruction format
// Main fetch-execute loop
// Task and function definitions
// Utility operations and functions
endmodule     // End of vespa processor module.
```

Figure 4.1. The overall structure of the VeSPA behavioral model.

4.1 Module definition

The overall organization of the VeSPA behavioral model is shown in Figure 4.1. The **module** statement introduced in chapter 2, begins the basic unit of a Verilog description. Recall that this statement consists of the **module** keyword followed by the name given by the Verilog programmer to the module. In this case, we chose the name *vespa*. An optional list of input and output signals to this module can follow the module name. There are no inputs and outputs for this high-level module, however. The **module** statement must end with a semicolon. Finally, the keyword **endmodule** is used to mark the end of the nearest preceding **module** definition. Notice that **endmodule** is NOT terminated with a semicolon.

Within this module, we declare all of the storage elements we previously defined in the ISA, and we use compiler directives to define easy-to-read names for the fields in the instruction format, for the opcodes, and so on. The main work performed by the processor to execute instructions is described in the main *fetch-execute* loop. This statement controls the operation of this behavioral model and, thereby, the flow of execution of the individual instructions of the machine language program being executed. *Functions* and *tasks* used within this loop also are defined in this module. These functions and tasks are used within the main loop to structure and simplify the Verilog description much as functions and subroutines are used in programming languages. Each of these components of the behavioral model are described in the following sections.

4.2 Instruction and storage element definitions

4.2.1 Parameters

As in any form of programming, it is considered good practice to parameterize constant values as much as possible. That is, a name is given to a constant and then this name is used throughout the program instead of the value itself. This technique allows the value of the constant to be changed in only one location and then have the modified value automatically propagated to every location where it is used in the program. In Verilog, the **parameter** statement is used to assign a value to a symbolic name.

We define three parameters in the VeSPA behavioral model:

```
parameter    WIDTH = 32;            // Datapath width.
parameter    NUMREGS = 32;          // Number of registers in the ISA.
parameter    MEMSIZE = (1 << 13);   // Size of the memory actually
                                    // simulated. Address range is
                                    // 0 to (2^13 - 1).
```

The **parameter** keyword begins the statement followed by one or more definitions of the form *name = constant expression*. Multiple definitions within one parameter statement must be separated with commas. The statement is terminated with a semicolon.

In the first parameter statement, we define the width of the registers and corresponding data paths to be 32 bits. The second statement defines the number of registers to be 32, as we previously defined in the ISA. We could easily change the data width of the processor to 16 bits, for instance, by changing this single statement. Similarly, we could increase the number of registers in the processor by changing the second statement. Note, however, that changing the number of registers also would require us to redefine the instruction format to accommodate the additional bits required to address the increased number of registers. Thus, this change would have ramifications far beyond this single statement.

The third parameter statement is slightly more complex than the other two. In this statement, we are defining how much of the processor's memory we really want to simulate. Recall that, in the ISA definition, we said that the memory consists of 2^{32} bytes where each consecutive address points to a single byte. However, it would be impractical to simulate such a large memory system. Instead, we use this parameter statement to determine what subset of this memory we should simulate. The Verilog expression (1 << 13) is evaluated at compile-time to produce a constant value to assign to the parameter name MEMSIZE. The operator << shifts the bit pattern on the left-hand side by the number of bit positions specified on the right-hand side. The statement thus shifts the value 1 left 13 times, which is equivalent to computing 2^{13}. Consequently, this parameter statement causes the value 8192 to be substituted for the name MEMSIZE wherever it appears in the remainder of this Verilog program.

4.2.2   Register declarations

After defining these parameters, we declare all of the storage elements that are defined in the ISA.

```
reg[7:0]          MEM[0:MEMSIZE-1];    // Byte-wide main memory.
reg[WIDTH-1:0]    R[0:NUMREGS-1];      // General-purpose registers.
reg[WIDTH-1:0]    PC;                  // Program counter.
reg[WIDTH-1:0]    IR;                  // Instruction register.
reg               C;                   // Condition code bit.
reg               V;                   // Condition code bit.
reg               Z;                   // Condition code bit.
reg               N;                   // Condition code bit.
reg               RUN;                 // Execute while RUN=1
```

The basic Verilog storage element is a single-bit register called a reg. It can be extended into a vector of bits to produce a multibit register that can be referenced using a single name. The statement reg[WIDTH-1:0] PC;, for instance, declares a register WIDTH bits wide. The most-significant bit can be referenced as PC[WIDTH-1] with the least-significant bit referenced as PC[0]. The expression PC[4:2] extracts a field consisting of bits 4, 3, and 2 from the register PC. The Verilog compiler interprets a value in a **reg** vector as an unsigned integer.

A register definition can be extended to a two-dimensional array of registers by subscripting the name assigned to the register. For instance, the statement

```
reg[7:0]  MEM[0:MEMSIZE-1];
```

from above declares an array of registers called MEM, each of which is eight bits wide. This statement is used to declare the memory in the simulated VeSPA processor that is included within this behavioral model. A single register within this array is referenced using MEM[96], for example. It is not possible to reference a single bit from this array of registers, however. To pull out a single bit or field of bits, MEM[96] would have to be assigned to another register, such as IR.

The remainder of the registers included in this list of declarations are those we defined as part of VeSPA's ISA, except for the registers IR and RUN. The IR register is the *instruction register*. This register is not directly accessible to the assembly language programmer and so was not defined in the ISA. However, every processor needs an IR to hold the most recent word read from memory that is the current instruction being executed. Signals from the IR will be used to select which operation is performed, which registers will be used as the input operands, and so on. The RUN register, in contrast, is declared simply as a convenience for the behavioral model. It is used as a flag register and is reset by the HLT instruction to signal the end of the simulation.

We also define the following registers:

```
reg[WIDTH-1:0]  op1;     // Source operand 1.
reg[WIDTH-1:0]  op2;     // Source operand 2.
reg[WIDTH :0]   result;  // Result value.
```

These are not 'architected' registers, however. Similar to the RUN register, they are defined specifically for the behavioral model to assist in calculating the condition codes. Note, for instance, that the result register is one bit wider than the processor WIDTH defined previously. This extra bit stores the carry-out value generated by the arithmetic operations. It is subsequently used to set the C bit of the condition code bits. However, it is not defined in the ISA. Consequently, it may or may not exist in a final implementation. In any case, the assembly language programmer cannot count on its existence since the hardware implementer may choose to throw it out completely in the final implementation.

4.2.3   Instruction field and opcode definitions

To make the Verilog code readable by a human, we define an easy- to-read identifier for each opcode in the ISA. We use the 'define statement for this purpose, as shown in the following Verilog statements.

```
'define NOP    'd0
'define ADD    'd1
'define SUB    'd2
'define OR     'd3
'define AND    'd4
'define NOT    'd5
'define XOR    'd6
'define CMP    'd7
'define BXX    'd8
'define JMP    'd9
'define LD     'd10
'define LDI    'd11
'define LDX    'd12
'define ST     'd13
'define STX    'd14
'define HLT    'd31
```

In the above statements, the 'define is being used in a manner similar to the parameter statement. However, the parameter statement is used to assign a constant value to a symbolic name. Since the value in the parameter statement is computed at compile-time, it can contain arbitrarily complex expressions. The 'define, in contrast, performs a strict textual substitution[1]. For instance, after the above 'define statements are encountered, the compiler will insert the text 'd31 wherever it encounters the text 'HLT.

---

[1] This textual substitution is essentially the same as the operation of the #define command in the C programming language.

The backquote character (') is used in Verilog to identify *compiler directives*. A compiler directive is a command to the compiler to perform some operation that will remain in effect throughout the compilation, or until the directive is specifically turned off. The 'undef directive removes a previous definition. For example, 'undef HLT will disassociate the text 'd31 from the text HLT.

The forward quote (') in the above definitions is used to indicate the numeric base in which a constant is to be interpreted. The bases available in Verilog are:

- 'd – decimal
- 'h – hexadecimal
- 'b – binary
- 'o – octal

The base identifier is not case sensitive so that 'd or 'D can be used for decimal, 'h or 'H can be used for hexadecimal, 'b or 'B can be used for binary, and 'o or 'O can be used for octal.

A *size* specification can optionally precede the base identifier to indicate the number of bits that should be used to represent the constant value. For example,

- 4'hC is a four-bit constant with the value 12.
- 8'b0110 is an eight-bit constant with the value 6. If the value given is smaller than the size, the most significant bits are padded with zeroes.
- 2'b0110 is a two-bit constant with the value 2. When the specified size is too small for the given value, the most significant bits are simply truncated. Also note that spaces can appear between the size and base specifiers and between the base and the constant value.

In addition to relating easy-to-read names to the opcode values, it is useful to identify each of the conditional branch instructions with its corresponding binary pattern using the 'define, as follows:

```
'define BRA    'b0000
'define BNV    'b1000
'define BCC    'b0001
'define BCS    'b1001
'define BVC    'b0010
'define BVS    'b1010
'define BEQ    'b0011
'define BNE    'b1011
'define BGE    'b0100
'define BLT    'b1100
'define BGT    'b0101
'define BLE    'b1101
```

```
'define BPL      'b0110
'define BMI      'b1110
```

Finally, we give a symbolic name to each of the fields we defined in the instruction format.

```
'define OPCODE    IR[31:27]    // opcode field
'define rdst      IR[26:22]    // destination register
'define rs1       IR[21:17]    // source register 1
'define IMM_OP    IR[16]       // IR[16]==1 when source 2 is immediate
                               // operand
'define rs2       IR[15:11]    // source register 2
'define rst       IR[26:22]    // source register for store op
'define immed23   IR[22:0]     // 23-bit literal field
'define immed22   IR[21:0]     // 22-bit literal field
'define immed17   IR[16:0]     // 17-bit literal field
'define immed16   IR[15:0]     // 16-bit literal field
'define COND      IR[26:23]    // Branch conditions.
```

These definitions make it much easier to read the code that describes what each instruction does. Note that we can give different names to the same or overlapping fields from the IR. For instance, rst and rdst both refer to bits [26:22] of the IR. The reason for defining two different names for the same instruction bits is to make these names correspond to the fields we previously defined in the ISA for the different instructions.

4.3   Fetch-execute loop

The execution of machine instructions by a processor can be reduced to two basic steps. First, the next instruction to be executed is fetched from memory and stored in the IR. Next, the instruction is decoded and the indicated operation is performed. This process, which is called the *fetch-execute cycle*, then repeats for the next instruction. Recall that the PC (program counter) determines which instruction is executed next. Thus, the PC needs to be incremented at some point during this fetch-execute cycle to point to the next instruction in memory that will be executed.

The Verilog code needed to implement this type of fetch-execute cycle for VeSPA is shown below.

```
initial begin

  $readmemh("v.out",MEM);  // Read v.out file into MEM.

  RUN = 1;                 // RUN gets reset by the HLT instruction.
  PC = 0;                  // Start executing from address 0.
  num_instrs = 0;
```

```
while (RUN == 1)
  begin
    num_instrs = num_instrs + 1;  // Number of instructions executed.
    fetch;                        // Fetch the next instruction.
    execute;                      // Execute it.
    print_trace;                  // Print a trace of execution,
                                  // if enabled.

  end

  $display("\nTotal number of instructions executed: %d\n\n",
    num_instrs);
  $finish;                        // Terminate the simulation and exit.

end
```

The `initial` statement in a Verilog model is executed exactly once at simulation time 0. The statements between the `begin` and the `end` keywords will be executed in the order shown, as in any procedural programming language, such as C. The `initial` statement is useful for initializing constants at the start of a Verilog simulation, for instance. A module may have any number of `initial` statements. All of them will appear to execute once concurrently at the beginning of the simulation. Thus, the order of these statements is not important. In this behavioral model of VeSPA, however, the entire simulation will occur within this single `initial` statement bracketed by the `begin` and the `end` statements.

The first step performed in the simulation is to read the contents of a file called `v.out` using the `$readmemh` statement. The values read from this text file are stored into the previously defined array of registers we called MEM. It is assumed here that someone has written a program in the VeSPA binary machine language and has stored this program in text format in the file `v.out`. Typically, an assembler would be used to produce this file. We are using this `$readmemh` statement to simulate the operation of an operating system's loader function storing a program into the processor's memory prior to executing it.

The system task `$readmemh` reads a text file and stores it in the indicated memory beginning at the smallest memory index. The contents of the text file are assumed to be hexadecimal values. Alternatively, the `$readmemb` system task is available to read files that are in are assumed to be binary values. The contents of a file consisting of VeSPA machine language statements, for example, could look like this:

```
50 00 00 18
58 40 00 00
08 43 00 01
38 02 00 00
46 ff ff f4
f8 00 00 00
00 00 00 0a
```

Each line contains the four bytes that comprise one VeSPA instruction. Each of these values must be separated by by one or more spaces or tabs, or by a new line. The above file contains 28 eight-bit values expressed in hexadecimal. Notice that we cannot write all four bytes as a single hex value, such as `5000000f`. The problem with this format is that MEM was defined as a byte-wide memory. Thus, the values read by `$readmemh` must be single bytes.

It also is possible to specify a range of addresses in the `$readmemh` (or `$readmemb`) system task calls. For instance,

```
$readmemh("v.out",MEM, 32, 64)
```

would store the first 32 values read from `v.out` into MEM beginning at address 32 and continuing sequentially through address 64. Finally, addresses may be specified explicitly within the text file using the @ sign. Thus, a text file that contained

```
@0020 50 00 00 38
@0024 58 40 00 00
@0028 08 43 00 01
@002c 38 02 00 00
@0030 46 ff ff f4
@0034 f8 00 00 00
@0038 00 00 00 0a
```

would store the hex value 50 at `MEM[20]`, the value 00 at `MEM[21]`, the value 00 at `MEM[22]`, and so on. The addresses given in the file (i.e., the value following the @) are interpreted as hexadecimal values and do not have to appear in sequential order.

The next statement following the `$readmemh` statement simply sets the register RUN to 1 to indicate that the processor can begin executing. The RUN flag will be reset when the HLT instruction is executed. We also need to tell the processor the address in memory from which it is to begin executing. This is done by assigning 0 to the PC register. A consequence of this assignment is that anyone writing assembly language programs for this processor must ensure that the first instruction they want executed is located at address 0 in VeSPA's address space. We could change this requirement by assigning a different value to the PC at this point in the simulation. Many processors, for instance, assign all ones to the PC when the processor is reset. (The instruction at this address should be a jump to the start of the program.) The choice of starting addresses is arbitrary. However, whatever choice is made must be communicated to the assembly language programmers.

The statement `num_instrs = 0;` initializes an integer variable. This variable must have been previously declared using the statement

```
integer num_instrs;
```

Integer variables can be freely used in behavioral models to store signed integer values. Integer variables are typically a minimum of 32 bits, although some Verilog compilers may use more bits to represent the value. Bit vectors cannot be extracted from integers. Instead, the integer must be assigned to a variable that was declared as a `reg`. Type conversion between `reg`s and `integer`s is automatic when using an assignment statement. In this behavioral model of VeSPA, we use this integer variable to count the total number of instructions that are executed in the simulation.

After all of this initialization, we finally encounter the actual fetch-execute loop. The `while` statement will execute the immediately following statement as long as the condition within the parentheses is true. If the condition is already false at the start of the loop, the loop statement is not executed. Only a single statement can follow the `while`. If multiple statements are to be executed within the loop, they must be enclosed within the `begin` and `end` statements. In our simulation, the `while` loop will execute until the RUN flag is reset.

Within this fetch-execute loop, the first operation simply increments the count of the number of instructions executed. The next three statements, `fetch;`, `execute;`, and `print_trace;`, are calls to user-defined *tasks*. These tasks are like procedure calls in a high-level programming language. As we shall see later, tasks can have both input and output parameters. One of the most common uses of tasks is to allow the same piece of code to be called from multiple locations, possibly with different parameter values. Our goal in using tasks within this fetch-execute loop, though, is simply to make the code easier to read. We will define the operations performed in each of these tasks in the following sections.

The simulation of the processor ends with the system-defined `$display` and `$finish` tasks. The names of all system-defined tasks in Verilog begin with a $. The `$display` statement is Verilog's primary system-defined task for printing results. The syntax for this task is as follows:

```
$display("format specification", arguments);
```

As can be seen in the above fetch-execute loop, the `format specification` for the `$display` task is very similar to that used in the C programming language. The following formats can be specified in Verilog:

```
%b — binary value
%c — single ASCII character
%d — decimal value
%h — hexadecimal value
%m — a hierarchical name
%o — octal value
%s — string of ASCII characters
%t — Verilog-defined global time value
%v — signal strength value of a net
```

The format specifier following the percent character (%) is not case-sensitive. As in C, the following escape sequences can be used to print special characters.

```
\n — newline
\t — tab
%% — the % character
\" — the " character
\\ — the \ character
```

The `$display` task always prints to the standard output and ends by printing a newline character. The `$write` task is the same as the `$display` task except that it does not automatically print a newline. Furthermore, if no format specifier is given for a particular argument, both the `$display` and `$write` tasks print the value as if it were a decimal value. Similarly, the `$displayb`, `$displayh`, and `$displayo` tasks assume unspecified values to be binary, hexadecimal, and octal, respectively. These tasks have corresponding `$writeb`, `$writeh`, and `$writeo` tasks.

The `$finish` task terminates the simulation and causes the simulator to exit. A similar `$stop` task also terminates the simulation. However, this task causes the simulator to enter an interactive mode instead of returning control to the operating system.

4.4 Fetch task

We define the `fetch` task to read the value in memory currently being pointed to by the PC and then store that value in the IR. This is the next instruction to be executed by the VeSPA processor being simulated.

A task definition in Verilog begins with the `task` keyword. This is followed by the name of the task and terminated with a semicolon. The task's parameters are declared next. If the task does not have any parameters, nothing needs to be declared. A single statement that comprises the body of the task follows. The task is terminated with the `endtask` keyword. If more than one statement is needed within the task, they must be enclosed within a `begin-end` pair. A task must be defined within an enclosing `module` declaration.

The `fetch` task for VeSPA is defined as follows:

```
task fetch;
  begin
    IR = read_mem(PC);
    PC = PC + 4; // PC points to the next instruction to be executed
  end
endtask
```

The `read_mem` statement in this task is an example of a Verilog *function*. A function is similar to a task except that it is required to have at least one input and it returns exactly one value. Furthermore, a function is not allowed to call other tasks, and it cannot contain any delays. In this `fetch` task, the `read_mem` function is used to return the four-byte value in memory pointed to by the address that is its single argument. We encapsulate the actual operation of the memory in this function since the memory will be accessed by several instructions in the simulated instruction set. Furthermore, this encapsulation allows us to change the memory interface by changing only this single function. As long as the function continues to return a four-byte value and takes the 32- bit address as an input, no other changes should be needed in the code.

This instruction `fetch` task also is a good place to increment the PC by one instruction. Recall that each memory address was defined in the ISA to point to a single byte. However, each instruction is four bytes. Thus, incrementing by one instruction is equivalent to incrementing the PC by 4, as is done in this task.

4.4.1 Memory interface

At first glance, it would seem that the memory interface should be nothing more than a simple assignment statement. For instance, it would seem that the assignment

```
IR = MEM[PC];
```

should move the value in MEM at the address pointed to by the PC register into the IR. However, in defining the memory interface, we suddenly find that we are confronted with a choice that impacts the ISA.

The problem is that MEM is defined as an array of eight-bit wide registers while the IR is a 32-bit wide register. Somehow we must compose the eight-bit values in MEM into an appropriate 32-bit value to store into IR. And this is precisely what impacts the ISA definition.

We have two possible options. A given byte address x could store the least-significant byte of the 32-bit word, with address $x+1$ storing the next significant byte, $x+2$ storing the next byte, and $x+3$ storing the most-significant byte. Alternatively, this order could be reversed so that address x stores the most-significant byte up through the least-significant byte in address $x+3$.

The choice between these two options determines the *endian-ness* of our processor. A *big-endian* machine has the most significant byte (i.e., the 'big end' of the 32-bit value) stored at the lowest memory address. A *little-endian* machine, on the other hard, stores the least-significant byte (i.e., the 'little end') at the lowest memory address. Which option to choose is mostly irrelevant, except when transferring data between machines with different endian-ness, and when manipulating individual bits within a word. Since compilers and assemblers generate machine instructions, which requires manipulating the bits within the words, they must know the endian-ness of the machine. Thus, we must specify the endian-ness as part of the ISA definition.

Processors using both byte orderings exist. The Intel x86 family of processors uses a little-endian ordering, while the Sun SPARC, PowerPC, and 68000 families all use a big-endian ordering. We arbitrarily choose a big-endian ordering for VeSPA. This choice leads to the following definition for the `read_mem` function.

```
function [WIDTH-1:0] read_mem;
  input [WIDTH-1:0] addr;           // the address from which to read

  read_mem = {MEM[addr],MEM[addr+1],MEM[addr+2],MEM[addr+3]};

endfunction    // read_mem
```

The `function` keyword identifies the start of the function definition. The expression between the square brackets, `[WIDTH-1:0]`, specifies the size of the value that will be returned by the function. If no size is specified, it defaults to a single bit returned value. This declaration is followed by the function name. One or more `input` statements are used to declare the size of the inputs to the function, along with the names by which they are referenced within the function. The order of these input declarations corresponds to the order of the parameters when the function is called. A value is returned from a function by assigning the value to be returned to the function name.

The four bytes read from the `MEM` array in the `read_mem` function are composed into a single 32-bit value using the curly brackets (`{,}`). These brackets are the *concatenation* operator. In addition to concatenating groups of bits to compose larger values, concatenation can be used with *replication* in the format

```
{number of repetitions {expression, expression, ...}}
```

For example,

```
{4{3'b101}}
```

would produce the value 101101101101.

Notice that the order in which the individual values read from the `MEM` array are concatenated in the above function makes VeSPA a big-endian machine. If we had thought about it earlier, we would have defined the endian-ness of the machine as part of the ISA definition. However, this turns out to be one of those details that is easy to overlook. One of the advantages of developing this type of behavioral simulation model is that we are forced to precisely specify all of these types of details that will influence the ISA specification.

4.5   Execute task

The `execute` task is where the real work of the processor is performed. As with the `fetch` task, this task takes no inputs and produces no outputs. The execution of the VeSPA instructions is simulated by the changes they make to the processor's state, including the architectural registers, the condition code bits, and the memory.

   As shown below, the body of the `execute` task consists of a single `case` statement.

```
task execute;
  begin

    case ('OPCODE)

      'ADD: begin
        if ('IMM_OP == 0)
          op2 = R['rs2];
        else
          op2 = sext16('immed16);
        op1 = R['rs1];
        result = op1 + op2;
        R['rdst] = result[WIDTH-1:0];
        setcc(op1, op2, result, 0);
      end

      'AND: begin
        if ('IMM_OP == 0)
          op2 = R['rs2];
        else
          op2 = sext16('immed16);
        op1 = R['rs1];
        result = op1 & op2;
        R['rdst] = result[WIDTH-1:0];
      end

      'XOR: begin
        if ('IMM_OP == 0)
          op2 = R['rs2];
        else
          op2 = sext16('immed16);
        op1 = R['rs1];
        result = op1 ^ op2;
        R['rdst] = result[WIDTH-1:0];
      end
```

```
'BXX: begin
   if (checkcc(Z,C,N,V) == 1)
      PC = PC + sext23('immed23);
end

'CMP: begin
   if ('IMM_OP == 0)
      op2 = R['rs2];
   else
      op2 = sext16('immed16);
   op1 = R['rs1];
   result = op1 - op2;
   setcc(op1, op2, result, 1);
end

'HLT: begin
   RUN = 0;
end

'JMP: begin
   if ('IMM_OP == 1)      // If jump-and-link operation, the old PC
      R['rdst] = PC;      // value must be saved before it is lost.
   PC = R['rs1] + sext16('immed16);
end

'LD: begin
   R['rdst] = read_mem (sext22 ('immed22));
end

'LDI: begin
   R['rdst] = sext22('immed22);
end

'LDX: begin
   R['rdst] = read_mem(R['rs1] + sext17('immed17));
end

'NOP: begin
end

'NOT: begin
   op1 = R['rs1];
   result = ~op1;
   R['rdst] = result[WIDTH-1:0];
end

'OR: begin
   if ('IMM_OP == 0)
      op2 = R['rs2];
   else
      op2 = sext16('immed16);
   op1 = R['rs1];
```

```
      result = op1 | op2;
      R['rdst] = result[WIDTH-1:0];
    end

  'ST: begin
      write_mem(sext22('immed22),R['rst]);
    end

  'STX: begin
      write_mem(R['rs1] + sext17('immed17),R['rst]);
    end

  'SUB: begin
      if ('IMM_OP == 0)
        op2 = R['rs2];
      else
        op2 = sext16('immed16);
      op1 = R['rs1];
      result = op1 - op2;
      R['rdst] = result[WIDTH-1:0];
      setcc(op1, op2, result, 1);
    end

  default: begin
      $display("Error: undefined opcode: %d",'OPCODE) ;
    end

  endcase      // OPCODE case
  end
endtask
```

The basic format of a case statement is

```
case(case-expression)
  expression-1 : statement-1
  expression-2 : statement-2
  expression-3 : statement-3
  ...
  default: default-statement
endcase
```

The case statement, which is similar to the switch statement in C, provides a branching capability in Verilog in which one of several possible destinations can be selected. When the case statement is executed, the case-expression is first evaluated. This value then is compared to each of expression-1, expression-2, and so on. The statement following the colon (:) in the first expression that matches the value computed in the case-expression is then executed. If none of the expressions match, the default-statement is executed. The default statement is actually optional. However, it is good programming practice to always include a default option.

In our simulation of VeSPA, the case expression is simply the value 'OPCODE, which we previously defined as the field of bits in the IR that contain the opcode. The value of these bits from the IR is compared with each of the previously defined opcodes. The statements associated with the matching opcode, which are bracketed in a begin-end block, then are executed. The default condition catches the situation in which the processor tries to execute an undefined opcode.

The statements associated with each opcode determine the operations that will be performed on the state of the VeSPA processor when that opcode is executed. These operations are an almost literal translation of the operations we defined as part of the ISA in Chapter 3. (Also see Appendix A for a concise summary of each instruction's operation.)

The operation of the arithmetic and logical instructions all follow the same basic pattern. First, the immediate operand bit, 'IMM_OP, is checked to determine if the second operand is in one of the registers. This check is performed with an if statement. The conditions allowed in an if statement are the same as those in the C language:

```
==  − equal to
<=  − less than or equal to
>=  − greater than or equal to
<   − less than
>   − greater than
!=  − not equal to
```

If the condition evaluates to true, which is indicated by a nonzero value, the statement immediately following the if is executed. Otherwise, the statement following the else is executed. Nesting of if-else statements is allowed. Each else statement is always associated with the closest if that does not have a corresponding else.

The condition being evaluated in the VeSPA simulation is 'IMM_OP == 0. If this condition is true, that is, if this bit is equal to 0, the second operand for this instruction is taken from the register pointed to by 'rs2, which is one of the previously defined bit fields in the IR. If this condition evaluates to false, however, the operand has been specified as an immediate value and is taken from the appropriate 16-bit immediate field of the IR.

The function sext16 is used to sign-extend this 16-bit value into an appropriate WIDTH-bit value as follows (recall that WIDTH was previously defined to be 32 bits for this processor):

```
function [WIDTH-1:0] sext16;    // 16-bit input
  input [15:0] d_in;              // the bit field to be sign extended

  sext16[WIDTH-1:0] = { {(WIDTH-16){d_in[15]}} ,d_in};

endfunction      // sext16
```

This function uses the replication operator to duplicate the most-significant bit of this 16-bit value, which is its sign bit, 16 (i.e., WIDTH-16) times. The concatenation operator then is used to prepend the sign-extension field to the 16-bit input value to produce the full 32-bit value desired. This final 32-bit value is assigned to the function name to return the value to the calling location. We define the functions sext17, sext22, and sext23 to sign-extend input values of other sizes in a similar way.

After the two operands have been loaded into the op1 and op2 registers, the desired arithmetic or logical operation is performed and the result is stored in the result register. Recall that the result register was declared to be one bit wider than the WIDTH parameter to allow the storage of the carry-out bit of an ALU operation. Consequently, when the contents of this register are written to the appropriate register in the register file, identified with the 'rdst field, only the lower bits are used. This assignment of the larger width value to the smaller width register is performed with the statement R['rdst] = result[WIDTH-1:0];. Notice that the bit selection operator is used to extract the lower 32-bits from the result register. Finally, the setcc function is used to set the condition code bits for those instructions that were defined in the ISA as affecting the condition codes. The operation of the setcc function is detailed in Section 4.6.

Notice that the operations for the CMP instruction are exactly the same as those for the SUB instruction. The only difference is that the CMP instruction never stores its result. Its only impact on the processor's state is to change the value of the condition code bits (the PC also gets automatically updated when this instruction is executed, of course).

The operation of the branch instruction, BXX, in this behavioral model is quite simple. First, the checkcc function, which is described in detail in Section 4.6, is called to check the outcome of the specific condition being tested. If the returned value is a 1, indicating that the condition was true, the PC is loaded with the current value of the PC plus the sign-extended branch offset stored in the immediate field in the IR. This change to the PC register causes the program to fetch the next instruction to be executed from the branch target address. If the condition evaluates to false, however, no changes are made to the PC. The result is that the next instruction executed is the instruction immediately following the branch.

The JMP instruction operates in a similar fashion, except that no condition is checked. Instead, the PC always is updated with the sum of the address stored in the jump target register indicated with the 'rs1 field, and the sign-extended offset value stored in the immediate field in the IR. The `if` statement in this instruction is used to determine whether the old PC value needs to be saved in the link register specified by the 'rdst field. Recall that this old PC value is pointing to the instruction following the JMP as the JMP is being executed.

In the LDI instruction, the value stored in the destination register specified by the 'rdst field is obtained by sign-extending the immediate value stored in the IR. The operation of the LD instruction appears to be quite similar, except that the sign-extended value is used as the memory address in the `read_mem` function. Notice that this is the same `read_mem` function described in Section 4.4.1 when we discussed the `fetch` function. The LDX instruction also accesses the memory using the `read_mem` function. For this instruction, however, the memory address is computed as the sum of the value stored in the operand register specified by the 'rs1 field and the sign-extended immediate value in the IR.

The operations of the two store instructions, ST and STX, parallel the operations of the LD and LDX instructions. These instructions use the following `write_mem` task to access the memory, however.

```
task write_mem;
  input [WIDTH-1:0] addr;      // Address to which to write.
  input [WIDTH-1:0] data;      // The data to write.

  begin

  {MEM[addr],MEM[addr+1],MEM[addr+2],MEM[addr+3]} = data;

  end

endtask                        // write_mem
```

We use a task to write to memory instead of a function since we do not need to return any values. Instead, this task takes the address and the value to be written to memory as its input parameters. The assignment statement simulates the write of the 32-bit `data` value to four consecutive bytes in the MEM array in big-endian order.

The only operation performed by the HLT instruction in this behavioral model is to reset the RUN flag to 0. This action causes the condition being tested in the `while` statement in the fetch-execute loop to fail when the `execute` task returns. This change in the RUN flag prevents any more instructions from being fetched and executed.

The NOP instruction makes no changes to the processor's state, other than allowing the PC to be updated to point to the next instruction to be executed.

Finally, the `default` condition in this `execute` task prints out a message if the VeSPA processor attempts to execute an undefined opcode. We could cause the simulation to terminate at this point by inserting a `$stop` or `$finish` statement in the `default` case. However, we instead decide to let the simulation continue with the execution of the next instruction.

4.6   Condition code tasks

The VeSPA behavioral model uses one task and one function to interface with the condition code bits. The `setcc` task is called by those instructions that set the condition code bits. As seen in the following task definition, this task takes as inputs the two input operands and the corresponding result produced by the ALU. Additionally, it takes a single bit input, `subt`, to indicate that the operation performed was a subtraction.

```
task setcc;
  input [WIDTH-1:0] op1;         // Operand 1.
  input [WIDTH-1:0] op2;         // Operand 2.
  input [WIDTH   :0] result;     // The calculated result value.
  input subt;                    // Set if the operation was a subtraction.
                                 // In this case, the sign bit of op2
                                 // must be inverted to correctly
                                 // calculate the V bit.
  begin
    C = result[WIDTH];           // The carry out of the result.
    Z = ~(|result[WIDTH-1:0]);   // Result is zero if all bits are 0.
    N = result[WIDTH-1];         // Result is negative if the most
                                 // significant bit is 1.
    V = ( result[WIDTH-1] & ~op1[WIDTH-1] & ~(subt ^ op2[WIDTH-1]))
        | (~result[WIDTH-1] & op1[WIDTH-1] & (subt ^ op2[WIDTH-1]));
  end
endtask
```

The four condition code bits are set in this task according to the logic equations previously developed in Section 3.2.3 when defining the ISA. Thus, the C bit is the carry-out bit of the ALU, which has been stored in the most-significant bit of the 33-bit result register; the Z bit is the NOR of all of the bits in the result, excluding the carry-out bit; N is a copy of the sign bit of the result; and V is a function of the sign bits of the two input operands and the result. Note that the sign bit of the second operand is inverted using the exclusive-OR operator ($^\wedge$) if the operation performed was a subtraction.

While the `setcc` task sets the condition code bits, the `checkcc` function is used to test these bits based on the condition specified in a conditional branch instruction. A Verilog function is used for this checking since we need to return a value. The inputs to the `checkcc` function are the four condition code bits and the 'COND field of the IR. In the following function definition, we specify the four input bits explicitly. The

'COND has been defined globally, however, so there is no need to declare it as an input. In fact, the condition code bits also are globally accessible and so do not need to be declared as explicit inputs. However, the condition code bits are part of what is called the *architected state*. This terminology means that these bits are explicitly defined in the processor's ISA and will change as a consequence of the execution of instructions. The 'COND field, on the other hand, is a pseudonym for some of the IR bits. The form of the declaration used for **checkcc** emphasizes the fact that the primary inputs to this function are the architected state bits. The 'COND field determines what function of these input bits needs to be computed to evaluate the condition.

```
function checkcc;
    input Z;                      // The condition code bits.
    input C;
    input N;
    input V;

    begin
     case ('COND)

        'BRA: begin
           checkcc = 1;
        end

        'BNV: begin
           checkcc = 0;
        end

        'BCC: begin
           checkcc = ~C;
        end

        'BCS: begin
           checkcc = C;
        end

        'BVC: begin
           checkcc = ~V;
        end

        'BVS: begin
           checkcc = V;
        end

        'BEQ: begin
           checkcc = Z;
        end
```

```
    'BNE: begin
      checkcc = ~Z;
    end


    'BGE: begin
      checkcc = (~N & ~V) | (N & V);
    end


    'BLT: begin
      checkcc = (N & ~V) | (~N & V);
    end


    'BGT: begin
      checkcc = ~Z & ((~N & ~V) | (N & V));
    end


    'BLE: begin
      checkcc = Z | ((N & ~V) | (~N & V));
    end


    'BPL: begin
      checkcc = ~N;
    end


    'BMI: begin
      checkcc = N;
    end

  endcase           // COND case
 end
endfunction         // checkcc
```

The appropriate condition to test is selected using a case statement based on the 'COND field of the IR. In all cases, the function should return a 1 if the selected condition is true and a 0 if the condition is false. The logic equations needed to determine these outcomes are exactly those we developed in Table 3.3 in Section 3.2.3.

4.7   Tracing instruction execution

When debugging machine language programs written for the VeSPA processor, and when debugging the behavioral model itself, it is useful to have some facility to trace the execution of the program, and to monitor the contents of important registers, as it runs on the processor. We define the following print_trace function to perform this type of tracing.

```
task print_trace;
  integer i;
  integer j;
  integer k;

  begin

    'ifdef TRACE_PC
      begin
        $display("Instruction #:%d\tPC=%h\tOPCODE=%d", num_instrs,PC,
          'OPCODE);
      end
    'endif    // TRACE_PC

    'ifdef TRACE_CC
      begin
        $display("Condition codes: C=%b V=%b Z=%d N=%b", C,V,Z,N);
      end
    'endif // TRACE_CC

    'ifdef TRACE_REGS
      begin
       k = 0;
       for (i = 0; i < NUMREGS; i = i + 4)
         begin
         $write("R[%d]: ",k);
         for (j = 0; j <= 3; j = j + 1)
           begin
             $write(" %h",R[k]);
             k = k + 1;
           end
         $write("\n");
         end
      $write("\n");
      end
    'endif    // TRACE_REGS

  end
endtask
```

Recall from Section 4.3 that this `print_trace` task is called in the fetch-execute loop after each instruction is executed. By this point, you should understand enough about Verilog to be able to almost completely understand how this task operates.

One new Verilog statement in this task is the 'ifdef-'endif construct. This construct is used for conditional compilation. Specifically, if the name following the 'ifdef has been defined, the statements between the begin-end pair will be executed. If it has not been defined, the statements will be ignored. Thus, to turn on tracing of the PC as a VeSPA program is executed, we need the following statement near the top of the program:

```
'define TRACE_PC 1
```

Similar definitions will turn the tracing on for **TRACE_REGS** and **TRACE_CC**.

There is an 'else statement that can be used with the 'ifdef as shown in the following example:

```
'ifdef USE_64BIT
parameter   WIDTH = 64;
'else
parameter   WIDTH = 32;
'endif
```

The other new construct used in this task is the for loop. The syntax of the for loop is identical to that in the C language. That is,

```
for (start-value ; end-value ; increment)
```

4.8   Summary

The algorithmic behavioral model of the VeSPA processor as an almost literal translation from the ISA definition. This behavioral model can be used to execute programs written in VeSPA's machine language. In the next chapter, we describe the assembler used to translate programs written in VeSPA's assembly language into the machine language format that can be executed by this behavioral model simulation. Subsequent chapters will refine this behavioral model into a structural model that completely describes how a pipelined implementation of the processor can be constructed.

5 Building an assembler for VeSPA

In order to translate a sentence from English into French two things are necessary. First, we must understand thoroughly the English sentence. Second, we must be familiar with the forms of expression peculiar to the French language.

George Polya, How to Solve It, Princeton University Press, 1945.

5.1 Why assembly language?

The instructions that are actually executed by a processor are stored in memory as a sequence of binary numbers. When these numbers are fetched by the processor, they are executed by interpreting this *machine language* according to the steps specified in the instruction set architecture (ISA). It is possible to write programs directly in the binary 1s and 0s of a processor's machine language. However, it would be extremely tedious and error-prone since humans think in terms of symbols and higher-level languages. Consequently, we assign symbolic names to each of the instructions in the ISA, and to each of the registers and other memory elements that are accessible to a programmer. We then define a *syntax* which precisely describes how the various symbols can be composed into a complete program. These symbolic names and syntax define a complete programming language which is called an *assembly language*.

An *assembler* is a program that accepts as input a text file consisting of a sequence of alphanumeric characters that comprise a program written in a processor's assembly language. The output of the assembler is a machine language representation of the assembly language program that can be directly executed by the processor. The original textual format of the program is called the *source code*. The executable machine language is called the *object code*.

Most programmers will write their programs using a high-level language, such as C, Java, or Fortran. So why do we need to develop an assembler for a new processor? Perhaps the most important reason is that an assembly language is a good target language for the output of a compiler. That is, a compiler can translate the source code of a program written in a high-level language into the source code of the assembly language of the processor on which the program is to execute.

This processor's assembly language is called the *target* language of the compiler. The assembler then is used to translate this target assembly code into the final executable object code.

Of course, it is possible for the compiler to generate the machine language object code directly from the high-level language source code. However, it would have to duplicate most of the functions of the assembler anyway. Consequently, it may be easier for the compiler to translate from a high-level language into the assembly language of the target processor.

Another reason for programming in assembly language is that there may not yet be a compiler available for the processor. For example, when a new processor is being designed, a new compiler for this processor would have to be written at the same time. The processor designers often need to write some programs to test out the ISA specification on a simulator, for instance, before the compiler is available (see Chapter 8 for more information on writing these types of simple test programs). Thus, the processor designers are likely to make extensive use of the assembler.

Assembly language also is frequently used to write the software for performance-critical sections of an application program. Compilers generally are very good at producing consistently fast code for an entire program. However, a programmer who understands the intimate details of an application often can do a better job than a compiler of writing assembly code for important sections of the program. This is because the assembly code gives the programmer very fine control of the execution of the instructions. Furthermore, by understanding the specific needs of the application program, the programmer may be able to optimize the program in ways that would not be apparent to a compiler. As a result, it is not unusual to write an entire application in a high-level language. The performance-critical sections of the program then may be rewritten directly in assembly language. These assembly languages sections are linked to the portions written in the high-level language to produce the final, complete executable object file.

Finally, it may be necessary to program a portion of an application program directly in assembly code to access special features of a processor that cannot be expressed in a high-level language. For instance, a processor could be designed with special-purpose signal-processing or multimedia processing instructions. It may be difficult to find a compiler that can generate the assembly code needed to access these special-purpose instructions.

5.2   The assembly process

The conversion of an assembly language program into an equivalent machine language program can be performed with almost a one-to-one translation of the symbols representing the machine instructions into the corresponding machine code bit patterns. The translation process is slightly more complex than this direct conversion, however, since we wish to simplify the programmer's task by allowing symbolic names for variables and symbolic labels for the target addresses of branch instructions. For example, we want to allow the programmer to write a statement like ld r0,aaa to specify that the value at address aaa is to be loaded into register r0. However, we do not want to force the programmer to explicitly determine what the actual memory address of aaa is. Instead, the assembler should be able to figure out the address of this variable and automatically insert it into the appropriate field in the ld instruction.

Similarly, we want the ability to write a statement such as bne exit to specify the target of a branch using the symbolic name exit instead of the actual address. Again, the assembler will automatically determine the offset value that needs to be inserted into the appropriate field in the bne instruction.

5.2.1   Assembly language format

To prevent the assembler's translation job from becoming impossibly complex, assembly language programmers must conform to a specific *syntax*. This syntax specifies the order of the various components of an instruction that must be specified, the specific *mnemonic* names used for the operations, and so forth. Most assemblers require the statements in the source program to be written in the following format:

```
Label  Operation  Operands  Comment
```

The individual fields in each statement must be separated by appropriate white-space (i.e., blank space, tabs, and new-lines) to allow the assembler to distinguish each individual field. Appropriate use of white-space also can be used to enhance the readability of the program.

The Label field is optional. It is used to associate a symbolic name with the address at which this statement will ultimately get loaded into the processor's memory. The required Operation field is used to specify the actual operation that will be performed when the instruction is executed using the mnemonic name defined in the ISA. For example, this field may contain the mnemonic add or and to indicate the corresponding operation.

The symbolic names for an appropriate number of operands for the given operation are specified in the next field. Register operands are typically specified using a name such as r17 to indicate register number 17, for instance. Where appropriate for the given operation, labels also may be given in this field to symbolically specify an address in memory. An appropriate constant value may be given here for operations that will accept a literal value. The immediate addressing mode used to specify literal values is typically indicated by preceding the desired value with the # character.

Finally, the optional `Comment` field begins with a specific character, or sequence of characters, such as a semicolon. This field can contain any alphanumeric characters and is ignored by the assembler. It is used by the programmer to insert short comments that make the program more understandable to a human reader.

5.2.2   Two-pass assembler

The example VeSPA assembly language program in Figure 5.1 executes the instructions in a loop the number of times specified in the variable `count`. Notice that each of the statements in this program shows the basic structure described in the previous section. That is, it contains a field for an optional symbolic label followed by the operation mnemonic, the symbolic operands, and, finally, a comment. We will translate this example program by hand into the VeSPA machine language to demonstrate how the assembly process works.

We assume that this program has been stored in a file that can be read by the assembler one line at a time. Comments in this particular assembly language are identified with the semicolon character (;). Thus, the assembler will ignore the first five lines in this file.

As it is translating a program from assembly language into machine language, the assembler maintains a variable called the *location counter*, which we denote LC. The value of the location counter is the address in the target processor's memory space into which the next instruction assembled should be placed. LC will be incremented by an appropriate amount after each instruction is assembled so that the instructions will

```
;
; A test program that simply loops 'count' number of times.
; r0 = the value read from the variable 'count'
; r1 = the current iteration number
;
        .org 0          ; start the program at address 0
        ld r0,count     ; load the value of count into r0
        ldi r1,#0       ; initialize r1 to 0
back:   add r1,r1,#1    ; add one to the value in r1
        cmp r1,r0       ; compare iteration number (r1) to count (r0)
        ble back        ; loop if r1 <= r0
        hlt             ; otherwise, stop execution
;
; Define the storage locations
;
count:
        .word 0xA       ; number of times to loop (in hex)
```

Figure 5.1. An example of an assembly language program written for the VeSPA processor.

be placed in consecutive locations in memory. The statement `.org 0` is a command to the assembler telling it the address at which the instructions should be assembled. Thus, this statement forces the assembler to set LC = 0.

The next line read by the assembler is

```
ld      r0,count              ; load the value of count into r0
```

The assembler *parses* this line into four *tokens*, specifically, the symbolic opcode `ld`, the two operands `r0` and `count`, and the comma character (`,`). The semicolon and everything that follows it on the same line are ignored. The assembler now could try and generate the machine language code for this instruction. In particular, we defined the format for the `ld` instruction to be as shown in Figure 5.2. The opcode can be obtained by looking it up in a table. The five-bit value for the `rdst` field is known to be 00000 since one of the operands is the token `r0`, which specifies register 0. Filling in a value for the `immed22` field is slightly more difficult, however. This field should contain the address for the symbolic name `count`. Unfortunately, the assembler does not yet know the address to which this symbolic name will resolve since it has not yet seen this symbolic name defined. The address that should be associated with this name is not actually defined until near the end of the program in the statement that begins with `count:`. As a result, it cannot yet fill in this field in the instruction.

This problem of not knowing the addresses of symbolic names until after they have been encountered in the program is called the *forward referencing* problem. To resolve this problem of using a name in a program before it is defined, most assemblers adopt a *two-pass* approach. First, the entire program is read line-by-line by the assembler during which a *symbol table* is constructed. Each entry in the symbol table contains the alphanumeric name of a symbol and, once it is known, the memory address to which this name corresponds.

After the symbol table has been constructed, the assembler makes a second pass through the source code. Whenever it encounters a symbolic name during this pass, it can look up the corresponding address in the symbol table. This address then is used to generate the appropriate value to be inserted into the machine language code.

The assembler finds the definition of each symbol as follows. As it reads each line, it increments LC by the number of memory locations that will be needed to store the instruction specified in the line. Simultaneously, the assembler is looking

31 ⋯ 27	26 ⋯ 22	21 ⋯ 0
01010	rdst	immed22

Figure 5.2. The instruction format for the LD instruction.

for *labels*. A label is the definition of a symbolic name. In this assembly language, labels are a sequence of alphanumeric characters (i.e., a symbolic name) terminated with a colon (:). When it encounters a label, it makes an entry for the symbolic name in the symbol table. The address that corresponds to the symbol is the current value of LC. This value is stored in the symbol table along with the symbol itself.

In VeSPA, each instruction has a fixed length of four bytes. Thus, the addresses at which each instruction in the example program in Figure 5.1 will be assembled are those shown in Figure 5.3. On its first pass through this program, the assembler will find two symbols defined, the labels back: and count:. It will assign the value 8 to the symbol back and the value 24 to the symbol count. It then will begin the second pass through the source code with the symbol table shown in Figure 5.4.

During the second pass, the assembler has enough information to fill in the values for each field of every instruction. The final field in the ld instruction shown in Figure 5.2 can now be determined by looking up the value associated with count in the symbol table. This value is found to be 24. The complete machine language code for this instruction then is

```
01010 00000 0000000000000000000011000.
```

This value will be stored at address 0. When it is ultimately executed by the VeSPA processor, it will be interpreted as a load instruction that reads the contents of memory address 24 and puts the value into register r0.

```
            .org 0          ; start the program at address 0
0           ld r0,count     ; load the value of count into r0
4           ldi r1,#0       ; initialize r1 to 0
8 back:     add r1,r1,#1    ; add one to the value in r1
12          cmp r1,r0       ; compare iteration number (r1) to count (r0)
16          ble back        ; loop if r1 <= r0
20          hlt             ; otherwise, stop execution
24 count:
            .word 0xA       ; number of times to loop (in hex)
```

Figure 5.3. The addresses at which the instructions will be stored after the program in Figure 5.1 is assembled.

Symbolic name	Corresponding value
back	8
count	24

Figure 5.4. The contents of the assembler's symbol table at the start of the second pass through the program shown in Figure 5.1.

```
@0000 50 00 00 18
@0004 58 40 00 00
@0008 08 43 00 01
@000c 38 02 00 00
@0010 46 ff ff f4
@0014 f8 00 00 00
@0018 00 00 00 0a
```

Figure 5.5. The complete object file (in hex format) for the program in Figure 5.1 after it has been assembled. Note that the address of each instruction is shown in each line using the Verilog command @. This object code thus is ready to be read by an appropriate Verilog $readmemh() statement (see Section 4.3).

The remaining statements in the program are assembled into the final machine language in the same way. The final object code containing the machine language for this example program is shown in hex format in Figure 5.5.

5.3   VASM – the VeSPA assembler

The assembler we have developed for VeSPA is called VASM, for VeSPA ASeMbler. It is a simple two-pass assembler that accepts text files as input and produces an object file that can be read by the Verilog simulators of VeSPA developed in this book. Note that the machine code in this object file is actually stored as a series of ASCII characters representing the hexadecimal values of the machine language instructions. This format allows the object file to be viewed and modified with any text editor. It also is the format expected by the Verilog $readmemh() command.

The next section describes the VeSPA assembly language syntax, along with some useful assembler commands. (A programmer's summary of the syntax is given in Appendix B.) This is followed by a brief description of how each of the assembler passes accomplishes its tasks.

5.3.1   VASM syntax and assembler commands

Programs written in the VeSPA assembly language must conform to the standard structure described in Section 5.2.1, that is, an optional label followed by the operation and operands with an optional comment. White space (blanks, tabs, and new-lines) can be inserted freely anywhere in the input text to enhance the readability of the program. Note, however, that comments extend to only the end of a line – each new line is interpreted as a new assembly language statement. The number of operands that need to be specified is determined by the particular operation and addressing mode used.

Comments must be preceded by either a semicolon (;) or two adjacent slash characters (//). Any characters on a line that follow either of these symbols are ignored by the assembler. These two types of comment delimiters have identical meanings and can be used interchangeably. Immediate operands (i.e., literal values) are denoted using the pound character (#), such as #45. All values are assumed to be decimal unless they are preceded by the character sequence 0x to indicate a hexadecimal value. For example, 12 would be interpreted as the decimal value 12 while 0x12 would be interpreted as a hexadecimal value with the decimal equivalent of 18. Register operands are indicated by appending a number between 0 and 31 to the letter r or R, such as r23 or R13. The mnemonic names used for the operations are those listed in the ISA definition shown in Appendix A.

Symbolic names, also called *identifiers*, must begin with one upper- or lower-case letter. This letter may be followed by zero or more letters, digits, or the underscore character (_). Labels may not be the same as one of the mnemonics chosen for the operations, nor can they be the same as a register operand. For example, Exit_Here, b96, and a_0 are all valid identifiers, while add and r5 are not.

Label definitions are indicated by appending the colon character (:) to the end of an identifier, as in Exit_Here:. As mentioned previously, the value assigned to a symbolic name is the value of the location counter, LC, at the time the name is defined (using the colon). Note that a symbolic name can be defined only once in a program since each name can have only one value associated with it. It can be referenced multiple times, of course, but it can be defined only once.

In addition to the special meanings assigned to these characters, VASM has defined several special *assembler directives*. Ignoring lines that consist of only a comment, nearly every statement in an assembly language program gets converted into a corresponding machine language instruction. The exception to this rule is an assembler directive. Instead of causing the assembler to produce a machine instruction, a directive is a command to the assembler itself that will somehow alter the assembly process. The .org statement discussed previously is one example of an assembler directive. Recall that it forces the location counter to be set to the given value.

Three additional VASM directives are used to allocate space in the processor's memory for variables that will be accessed by the executing VeSPA program. These directives are: .byte, which reserves a single byte in memory and assigns it an initial value; .word, which reserves and initializes a word (four bytes) of memory; and .alloc, which reserves any number of words, but does not initialize them. All three of these directives force the location counter, LC, to be incremented by an appropriate value. In the case of .byte, the LC is incremented by 1, while .word causes it to be incremented by four bytes. Since .alloc allocates multiple words, the LC is incremented by four times the specified number of words. Finally, the .equ directive assigns a specific value to a symbolic name. This directive is frequently used to parameterize values in assembly language programs. See Appendix A for the precise syntax used by these directives.

5.3.2   Pass 1 – lexical analysis and parsing

VASM is a reasonably straightforward two-pass assembler. However, it reads the actual input file only once. During the first pass, each line of the input file is read and converted into an internal representation that is stored in the assembler's memory. The second pass then reads this internally-stored representation of the program instead of reading the actual input file again.

The first pass performs two types of operations as it reads the source code lines of the assembly language program – a *lexical analysis* combined with a *syntactical analysis*. The lexical analysis examines the sequence of characters one character at a time as the file is read in. It then groups these characters into meaningful chunks, called *tokens*. For example, the lexical analysis will group the sequence of characters add into a token for the add operation. Similarly, when the letter r or R is followed by a one- or two-digit number, the lexical analyzer will group these characters into a token for a register operand, such as r7.

These tokens then are passed to the *parser*, which performs the syntactical analysis of the program. This analysis checks to ensure that the tokens occur in the proper order, for instance, that an add token is followed by the required number of operands. The parser is responsible for generating the symbol table, inserting appropriate symbols and values into the table, and for maintaining the proper value of the location counter (LC). It also identifies label definitions, converts tokens representing numeric values into their actual binary values (which are stored in the symbol table), performs the operations specified by the assembler directives, and does a very limited amount of error checking.

The output of this first pass is the symbol table containing the values that correspond to all of the symbolic names used in the program. In addition, an internal data structure is constructed that contains the parsed representation of each input statement.

While it is certainly possible to write a program from scratch to perform this lexical analysis and parsing, a variety of tools have been written to simplify the process. In the case of VASM, we used the *lex* and *yacc* tools. These are very powerful tools frequently used by compiler developers to convert a program from a textual format into a representation that can be parsed and manipulated before generating the corresponding assembly or object code. It is beyond scope of this text to teach you all of the details about lex and yacc. The ideas are not particularly difficult to understand, although the terminology can get somewhat technical. Instead, we present a detailed example in Appendix B.4 showing how a new instruction can be added to VASM. This example should be sufficient to allow you to modify the assembler to suit your own needs.

5.3.3   Pass 2 – machine code generation

The second pass of the assembler scans through the internal representations of each assembly language program statement. As the statements are scanned, they are converted into the appropriate machine code. The values for all symbolic names can be obtained from the symbol table during this pass as the machine code is generated, as can the actual binary values of all numeric constants used as immediate values. This pass uses many bit manipulation operations to insert the appropriate values into each of the opcode and operand fields.

There is one small quirk in the generation of machine code for the conditional branch instructions that is worth mentioning here. The machine code for each type of branch instruction contains the same opcode in the first five bits of the instruction, as specified in the processor's ISA. The particular branch condition being tested by this instruction is specified in the next five bits. Finally, the remaining bits are used to specify the *branch displacement* or *offset* value. This displacement value is used to find the address to which the instruction should branch (i.e., the *branch target* address) if the condition being tested evaluates to TRUE.

Recall that the branch instructions use PC-relative addressing to specify the branch target address. With this type of addressing mode, the target address is found by adding the current value of the program counter to the sign-extended branch displacement value stored in the *immed23* field of the instruction. Consequently, the assembler must calculate the branch displacement for a branch instruction by finding the arithmetic difference of the current value of the location counter as it is generating the machine code and the value of the symbolic label used to identify the branch target address in the source code. However, we must remember that, when the branch instruction is actually executed, the program counter is pointing to the instruction *after* the branch instruction.

Thus, the assembler must calculate the branch displacement value such that at run-time, the value of the branch target address is [address_of (BRANCH_TARGET) = PC + 4 + OFFSET], where PC is the value of the program counter when the branch instruction is executed, OFFSET is the branch displacement value stored in the branch instruction, and address_of (BRANCH_TARGET)· is the address of the branch target. The offset value calculated by the assembler is found to be [OFFSET = address_of (BRANCH_TARGET) − (LC + 4)] where LC is the value of the PC when the branch instruction is executed, and address_of (BRANCH_TARGET) is the value stored in the symbol table for the branch target. Subtracting the additional 4 from this OFFSET corrects for the PC pointing to the next instruction. Notice that this correction value could be something other than 4 in a processor with variable length instructions.

The calculated OFFSET value must be truncated to 23 bits to fit into the immediate field available in the branch instructions. It is an error if the OFFSET is a value that cannot be represented in 23 bits.

5.4   Linking and loading

The VASM assembler described in this chapter is a simple two-pass assembler. It takes as input a single source code file and produces an object code file that can be directly read and executed by the simulated VeSPA processor. However, the world of assemblers can quickly become more complex when we start dealing with large programs and the assembly code produced by compilers for high-level languages.

Most large programs written in a high-level language are partitioned into several different files. Each file typically contains one or more procedures or subroutines that are components of the larger overall program. The routines in each of these files will be compiled and assembled separately. However, some of the variables and routines referenced within one file may actually be defined in another file. These types of references are called *external* references and are said to be *unresolved* when the file is assembled.

Before the program can be executed, each of the separately produced object files must be merged together into a single executable file. This merging is the job of a program called the *linker*. In the process of merging the the separate object files, the linker will attempt to resolve all of the external references. That is, when an external reference is found in one object file, the linker will search for the definition of the corresponding symbol in the other object files. In addition, the linker will search precompiled program *libraries* for external references made by the program to commonly used functions, such as input/output operations (e.g., `printf()` in C) and common mathematical functions. Any external references that are still unresolved after the linking process indicate that the programmer has made an error.

After the separate object files and library functions have been merged into a single executable file, a *loader* program must be invoked to transfer the executable object code from secondary storage into the processor's memory. Once it is in memory, the loader jumps to the first instruction in the executable file to begin the execution of the user's program.

Since there is no linker available for VeSPA, all programs assembled using VASM must be entirely contained within a single file. Furthermore, in the VeSPA simulator, the function of the loader is performed using the Verilog `$readmemh("v.out",MEM)` command. A loader would be necessary if an actual hardware implementation of VeSPA were built.

5.5   Summary

An assembly language is a human-friendly version of a processor's machine language. There is an almost one-to-one correspondence between the symbolic assembly language and the machine language to which it is translated. Assembly language is useful for writing programs for a processor before a complete high-level language compiler is available, and it makes a good target language for a compiler. It also is useful for space- and time-critical portions of application programs.

Assemblers typically use a two-pass process to translate a program's assembly language source code into the corresponding machine code. The primary function of the first pass is to determine the values (addresses) for all symbolic references. The second pass then uses these values, which have been stored in the symbol table, to generate the machine code. This chapter has described the VeSPA ASeMbler (VASM) as an example of a two-pass assembler.

6 Pipelining

If you were plowing a field, which would you rather use? Two strong oxen or 1024 chickens?

Seymour Cray (1925–1996), father of supercomputing

6.1 Instruction partitioning for pipelining

In Section 4.3 we learned that the execution of a processor instruction consists of two basic steps: fetching the instruction from memory, and then executing it. In the simplest implementation of a processor, the complete fetch-execute cycle would be completed for one instruction before the next one begins. We saw this type of one-instruction-at-a-time operation in the algorithmic behavioral model in Chapter 4. To speed up the execution of instructions, however, we can break the fetch-execute cycle into several simpler sub-operations. We then can overlap the execution of different instructions in an assembly line fashion where each step in the assembly line is dedicated to performing one specific operation for each instruction. This assembly line processing is called *pipelining*.

The first step in designing a pipeline for a processor is to determine the smaller sub-operations within the fetch-execute cycle that must be performed to execute an instruction. For the VeSPA processor, each instruction will perform some of the following sub-operations, although not all of the instructions will perform all of the operations:

- Fetch the instruction from memory.
- Increment the program counter.
- Fetch the operands from the registers.
- Compute a memory address.
- Read an operand from memory.
- Write a result to the memory or to a register.

The next step in designing the pipeline for VeSPA, or for any other processor ISA, is to determine how these individual operations should be partitioned into the different stages of the pipeline. Some of these operations must be executed sequentially for each instruction while others can be executed in parallel. For instance, incrementing the program counter to point to the next instruction to be executed can be completed in the same stage as fetching the current instruction from memory. However, the address used to fetch an operand from memory must be computed before the memory can be read.

A straightforward partitioning of these operations leads to the following five-stage pipeline:

1. Instruction fetch stage (IF).
2. Instruction decode/register fetch stage (ID).
3. Execution stage (EX).
4. Memory access stage (MEM).
5. Write-back stage (WB).

This partitioning produces the pipeline shown in Figure 6.1. The first stage in this pipeline, called the IF stage, reads an instruction from memory at the address being pointed to by the current value of the program counter. Concurrently in this stage, the program counter is incremented to point to the next instruction to be executed.

On the next clock cycle, the instruction enters the ID stage. The primary action in this stage is to decode the opcode bits to determine what operation the instruction will perform. In addition, the bits that specify the register operands are used to read the operands from the register. The branch target address also is computed in this stage. All of these operations are carried out in parallel. As a result, this stage may read values from the registers that turn out not to be needed, and may compute a branch target address that is never used. For instance, some instructions need only a single operand. However, two operands would be read since this stage is still decoding the opcode. Any values that are read or computed unnecessarily are simply ignored and not used in any subsequent pipeline stages.

After being decoded in the ID stage, the instruction advances into the EX stage. The opcode has been decoded by this stage, and the operand values have been read from the registers. This information is passed from the ID stage and is used to set up the ALU to actually compute the desired operation during this EX stage if the instruction is a register-to-register ALU operation, such as AND, ADD, and so on. If the instruction is a register-immediate operation, the sign-extended immediate value

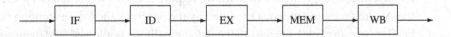

Figure 6.1. The basic pipeline structure consists of the following five stages: Instruction Fetch; Instruction Decode/register fetch; instruction **EX**ecution and effective address calculation; **MEM**ory access; register Write-Back.

is used as one input to the ALU with the other input being one of the operand values read in the ID stage. Finally, if the instruction is a load or store, this stage is used to compute the effective memory address.

Now that the desired operation has been computed in the EX stage, or the effective memory address has been determined, these values are passed to the MEM stage. This stage is dedicated to accessing the memory for load and store instructions. The effective address computed in the EX stage is used to read the desired location from memory for load instructions. For store instructions, on the other hand, the operand value read in the ID stage is written to memory at the given address. All other types of instructions pass through this stage without changing anything.

The final stage of the pipeline, WB, is where the values computed in the EX stage are finally written back to the destination register. The address of this register was previously determined in the ID stage and has been passed along through all of the intermediate stages. The value that is written back is either the value read from memory, if the instruction is a load, or the value computed in the EX stage. Store instructions do nothing in this stage since they have already completed their operation in the MEM stage.

6.2 Pipeline performance

With the pipeline partitioned into these five stages (Section 6.1), a single instruction will require five cycles to complete its execution. The real advantage of pipelining, though, is that, as an instruction moves from the first pipeline stage to the second, a new instruction can enter the first stage. As these two instructions move to their subsequent stages, another instruction enters the first stage, and so on, as shown in Figure 6.2. In this fashion, a new instruction can begin executing each cycle. Once the pipeline fills completely with instructions, one instruction will finish its execution every clock cycle, assuming that there is no interference between instructions (possible sources of interference are discussed later in Section 6.3). Thus, up to n instructions can be in various stages of execution simultaneously, where n is the number of stages in the pipeline.

The ideal speedup that could be produced by a pipelined processor can be determined as follows. If no overlapping of instructions is allowed in the pipeline, that is, if a new instruction is not allowed to enter the pipeline until the previous instruction has exited the pipeline, a single instruction would require n cycles to complete its execution. If there were I total instructions executed by the program, the total execution time would be $T_{no-pipe} = In$ cycles. On the other hand, if pipelining is allowed, and there are no inter-actions among the instructions, a new instruction can enter the pipeline each cycle. The first instruction would require n cycles to make its way through the pipeline and complete its execution. All of the remaining instructions would follow immediately

Clock Cycle	IF	ID	EX	MEM	WB
0	—	—	—	—	—
1	i	—	—	—	—
2	$i+1$	i	—	—	—
3	$i+2$	$i+1$	i	—	—
4	$i+3$	$i+2$	$i+1$	i	—
5	$i+4$	$i+3$	$i+2$	$i+1$	i
6	$i+5$	$i+4$	$i+3$	$i+2$	$i+1$
...	...	...	...	...	...

Figure 6.2. In clock cycle 0, the pipeline is initially empty. The first instruction, i, enters the pipeline in the IF stage during clock cycle 1. At the beginning of the next clock cycle, instruction $i+1$ enters the IF stage while i advances to the ID stage. On each subsequent cycle, new instructions continue to enter the IF stage as each instruction already in the pipeline advances one stage. As instructions complete, they exit the pipeline at the WB stage. With this five-stage pipeline, up to five instructions can be executing different portions of their *fetch-execute* cycles simultaneously.

behind this first instruction so that another instruction will complete its execution on every subsequent cycle. The total execution time for the fully pipelined configuration then is n cycles for the first instruction, plus $I-1$ cycles for the remaining $I-1$ instructions, giving $T_{pipe} = n + (I-1)$ cycles. The speedup of the pipelined processor compared to the unpipelined processor is the ratio of these two execution times:

$$Speedup = \frac{T_{no\text{-}pipe}}{T_{pipe}} = \frac{In}{n + (I-1)} = \frac{n}{1 + \frac{n-1}{I}} \qquad (6.1)$$

This speedup approaches n as the number of instructions executed in the program, I, becomes very large compared to n. Thus, the maximum possible speedup for a pipelined processor is equal to the number of stages in the pipeline.

Of course, we seldom achieve this ideal speedup since one instruction may need a result produced by an earlier instruction before it has reached the pipeline stage where the needed result has been computed. Limited hardware resources may further restrict an instruction from completing every cycle. Collectively, the restrictions on a pipelined processor's performance are due to *dependences* and *hazards*, which are discussed in the next section.

6.3   Dependences and hazards

As described in the previous section, an ideal pipeline can have n instructions in different stages of execution simultaneously, where n is the number of pipeline stages. In this ideal situation, one instruction can complete every cycle. The performance of real pipelines, however, is limited by interactions between instructions in the application program being executed. From the compiler's or programmer's point-of-view, we say that there are *dependences* between instructions that force the instructions to be executed in a particular order. Dependences that occur between instructions that try to execute in the pipeline at the same time can lead to *hazards* in the pipeline. These hazards then can limit the maximum performance that can be obtained from a pipelined processor.

6.3.1   Program dependences

Dependences are a consequence of how we write programs. In particular, some instructions *depend* on values produced by previous instructions, or they produce values needed by subsequent instructions. There are two fundamental types of dependences that arise in programs, *control dependences* and *data dependences*.

Control dependences

A control dependence exists from instruction x to instruction y when: 1) x is a branch instruction; and 2) whether or not y is executed depends on whether branch instruction x is *taken* or *not taken*. For example, consider the program code fragment shown in Figure 6.3, which has been extracted from some larger program. The instructions that follow the `ble` instruction are all control dependent on that branch since they will be executed only if the branch is not taken.

Except for the very first basic block[1] in a program, all instructions are control dependent on one or more branch instructions. These control dependences define the order in which instructions are to be executed. This order is preserved in a pipelined processor by ensuring that all instructions enter and exit the pipeline in the order in

```
        ld  r0,count    ; Instruction 1
        ldi r1,#0       ; Instruction 2
back:   add r1,r1,#1    ; Instruction 3
        cmp r1,r0       ; Instruction 4
        ble back        ; Instruction 5
        ld  r3,X        ; Instruction 6
        ldi r2,#3       ; Instruction 7
        add r2,r3,r2    ; Instruction 8
        sub r1,r2,r5    ; Instruction 9
        and r3,r5,r1    ; Instruction 10
```

Figure 6.3. A portion of a program extracted from some larger application program to illustrate control dependence.

---

[1] A basic block is a sequence of instructions that has no branches into or out of the block.

which they appear in the source code. Furthermore, the pipeline must be able to detect branch instructions and ensure that instructions that follow a branch are executed in the pipeline only when the branch direction is known.

Data dependences

Data dependences arise between instructions because of the way they use registers and access memory. There are three different types of data dependences, *flow* dependences, *anti*-dependences, and *output* dependences.

Flow dependences: A flow dependence exists from instruction *x* to instruction *y* when *y* needs a value produced by *x* before *y* can begin executing. In Figure 6.3, for example, there is a flow dependence from Instruction 8 to Instruction 9 through register r2. Flow dependences can chain through a sequence of instructions so that Instruction 10 also is said to be dependent on Instruction 8 since the and needs the value produced by the previous sub, which needs the value produced by the preceding add. Flow dependences are often called *true* data dependences since the dependent instruction cannot proceed any further in its execution until it has the value produced by the earlier instruction.

Anti-dependences: An anti-dependence occurs between two instructions when a following instruction writes to a register or memory location that first needs to be read by a preceding instruction. In Figure 6.3, Instruction 10 is anti-dependent on Instruction 8 since the add instruction must read the value in r3 before it is overwritten by the and instruction.

Output dependences: Two instructions have an output dependence when they both write to the same register or memory location. Instructions 3 and 9 in Figure 6.3, for example, both write to r1. As a result, Instruction 9 cannot complete its execution until Instruction 3 has completed, otherwise the instructions between 3 and 9 would read the wrong value from r1.

Anti- and output dependences are sometimes referred to as *name* dependences since the dependence exists only because one of the instructions reuses a register or memory location that was used by the previous instruction. However, there is no computed value that is being passed from one instruction to another. Thus, name dependences are not true dependences. In fact, by using a different register or memory location in one of the instructions, that is, by *renaming* the registers, these name dependences can be eliminated. They are simply a consequence of a programmer or compiler trying to reuse a storage location that has been used previously.

6.3.2   Pipeline hazards

Program dependences create *hazards* in the pipeline whenever the dependent instructions could both be in the pipeline simultaneously. The pipeline must detect these hazards and it must take appropriate steps to ensure that instructions do not actually interfere with each other. If dependent instructions are separated by a sufficient distance in the program, they will not cause a hazard in the pipeline.

The types of hazards that the pipeline must watch out for follow the types of program dependences described above. In particular, control or *branch hazards* can occur between instructions that share a control dependence, while *data hazards* are a consequence of data dependences. One additional type of hazard in a pipeline can occur when two instructions try to simultaneously use the same, limited hardware resource. This final type of hazard is called a *structural hazard*.

Branch hazards

A branch (or control) hazard occurs because, in most pipeline implementations, the outcome of a branch is not known until several cycles after a branch instruction has been fetched into the pipeline. However, the instructions that immediately follow the branch continue to be fetched into the pipeline. If the branch ultimately turns out to be *not taken*, then these instructions can continue their execution through the entire pipeline as normal. If the branch turns out to be *taken*, though, then these instructions should not be executed since they are on the *not taken* path of the branch.

For example, in the VeSPA ISA, branch instructions must test the condition code register to determine whether the branch should be taken or not. However, these condition codes cannot be checked until the pipeline figures out that the instruction actually is a branch instruction. This determination is made in the instruction decode (ID) stage, which is the second stage of the pipeline. After the branch instruction (Instruction 5) in Figure 6.3 moves from the IF stage to the ID stage, Instruction 6 will be automatically fetched into the IF stage. If the ble is taken, however, the target of this branch, Instruction 3, should be the next instruction fetched and executed, not Instruction 6.

Unfortunately, determining the outcome of the branch cannot be done until the ble has completed the ID stage. As a result, once the pipeline detects that the branch direction is *taken*, the pipeline's branch logic must flush the incorrect instructions out of the pipeline and begin fetching the instructions located at the branch target address. In this example program, it must reset the PC to begin fetching from Instruction 3. Figure 6.4 shows how the instructions from this example program would move through the pipeline when the branch direction turns out to be *taken*.

The nop instruction that gets inserted in Figure 6.4 introduces a one-cycle delay after every *taken* branch. These *pipeline bubbles* reduce the number of useful instructions that complete per cycle, which obviously reduces the processor's performance. The number of bubbles (i.e., nop instructions) that must be inserted after a branch is called the pipeline's *branch penalty*.

One technique for dealing with the branch penalty is to delay the action of the branch instruction for *n* cycles. That is, this *delayed branch* will always execute the

Cycle	IF	ID	EX	MEM	WB
k	ble back	cmp r1,r0	add r1,r1,#1	ldi r1,#0	ld r0,count
$k+1$	ld r3,X	ble back	cmp r1,r0	add r1,r1,#1	ldi r1,#0
$k+2$	add r1,r1,#1	nop	ble back	cmp r1,r0	add r1,r1,#1
$k+3$	cmp r1,r0	add r1,r1,#1	nop	ble back	cmp r1,r0
...	...	...	...	...	...

Figure 6.4. When the branch instruction from the example program shown in Figure 6.3 is executed in the five-stage pipeline, it is not known which direction the branch will take until it has moved through both the IF and ID stages. As a result, the instructions immediately following the branch continue to be fetched into the pipeline. If the branch turns out to be *not taken*, then these instructions should be executed normally. If the branch turns out to be *taken*, however, then the ld r3,X instruction that follows the branch should not be executed. Consequently, this instruction must be converted by the pipeline's branch hazard detection logic into a nop instruction in the ID stage during clock cycle $k+2$. During the same cycle, the add r1,r1,#1 instruction at the branch target address, that is, at the label back, is fetched.

n instructions that immediately follow the branch, regardless of whether the branch turns out to be *taken* or *not taken*. With a one-cycle branch delay, for instance, the instruction immediately following the branch is always executed. It is then up to the compiler to determine what instruction should be placed in this *branch delay slot*. If possible, the compiler would like to take an instruction from before the branch and insert it in the delay slot. Since the instruction will always be executed before the branch potentially changes direction, the program will execute exactly as if there was no branch delay slot and the instruction was never moved.

It is not always possible to find an instruction to insert in the delay slot, however, due to other program dependences. In this case, the compiler must explicitly insert a nop instruction into the delay slot. In the worst case, having the compiler insert the nop bubble is the same as having the hardware convert an incorrectly fetched instruction into a nop. In the best case, though, the branch penalty can be reduced to zero cycles by filling the delay slot with a useful instruction.

It is important to realize that a delayed branch operation will be visible to the compiler and the assembly language programmer. Thus, the specification of a delayed branch must become part of the ISA. In particular, the ISA must clearly state for every branch instruction whether it is a delayed branch, and the number of delay slots. The assembly language programmer or the compiler then must ensure that these delay slots are always filled with useful instructions, or with nops.

Data hazards

There are three different types of data hazards, which follow directly from the three different types of data dependences described in Section 6.3.1.

Read-after-write (RAW) hazards: A RAW hazard is a consequence of a flow dependence between instructions. The problem caused by a RAW hazard is that the result value produced by most instructions is not written to a register until the WB stage, which is the last stage in the pipeline. However, instructions read their operands from the registers early in the pipeline in the ID stage. As a result, if an instruction with a flow dependence on a preceding instruction follows too closely in the pipeline, it will read the old value in the register. What it really should be reading, though, is the new value that is being produced by the instruction on which it is flow dependent. The pipeline must detect this type of hazard and take corrective action to ensure that the dependent instruction does in fact read the appropriate value.

Write-after-read (WAR) hazards: WAR hazards occur because of anti-dependences. The potential problem is that a subsequent instruction will over-write a value in a register or in memory before the preceding instruction has a chance to read the old value. WAR hazards do not cause problems in most pipeline implementations, however, since register values are read early in the pipeline in the ID stage while register values are written in the last stage. This separation ensures that each instruction will read the most current values from the registers eliminating the need for the pipeline to check for WAR hazards.

Write-after-write (WAW) hazards: Output dependences lead to WAW hazards. The potential problem with WAW hazards is that the following instruction will over-write the register or memory location before the preceding instruction. This incorrect write order would leave the old value in the storage location thereby corrupting the computation of any subsequent instructions that need to read from this storage location. WAW hazards can occur only in pipelines that allow multiple stages to write to the registers or memory, or that allow instructions to execute out of order. In the simple five-stage pipeline discussed in this chapter, only instructions in the WB stage are allowed to write to the registers. Furthermore, instructions must pass through the pipeline in program order. As a result, WAW hazards can never occur in this pipeline.

Structural hazards

Structural hazards occur in a pipeline when two or more instructions try to simultaneously access some hardware resource beyond its capabilities. For instance, a structural hazard would exist if two instructions both try to read from memory simultaneously, but the memory has only one read/write port available. In this situation, one of the instructions would have to wait for the other to complete before it can proceed. Alternatively, the memory could be changed to allow multiple simultaneous reads and writes.

This type of structural hazard with memory is actually a common problem in pipelined processors. It can occur frequently because an instruction must be fetched from memory on every cycle. Additionally, there could be a load or store instruction in the MEM stage trying to read or write memory at the same time. Because of this conflict, most pipelines separate the top-level memory cache into a data cache and an instruction cache. The instruction cache is accessed on every cycle to feed instructions into the pipeline. Any load or store instructions then can access the separate data cache in the MEM stage without interfering with the instruction fetch stage. (See Section 7.5 for more discussion of caches.)

6.4 Dealing with pipeline hazards

Special logic in the pipeline can be used to detect hazards between instructions. If a hazard is detected, the pipeline must take some appropriate action to ensure that the program will still produce the correct results. The simplest and most straightforward action the pipeline can take is to stall all of the instructions fetched after an instruction that is the source of hazard. This instruction, and all of those fetched ahead of it, are allowed to continue through the pipeline. After they complete their execution, the stalled instructions are allowed to continue executing. This stalling operation is called a *pipeline interlock*.

Separating the instructions in this way ensures that the dependent instruction in a RAW hazard, for instance, obtains the correct value from the register. Similarly, this stalling can correct a structural hazard or a branch hazard by making sure that the conflicting instructions no longer conflict. The pipeline inserts nop instructions between the instruction that is the source of the hazard and the following stalled instructions because some instruction (i.e., the nop) must continue to flow through the pipeline stages.

Inserting these pipeline bubbles obviously reduces the performance of the pipeline compared to its potential ideal performance. Other more sophisticated techniques can be incorporated into the pipeline to eliminate the need to insert bubbles. For instance, *forwarding* logic can be used to compensate for RAW hazards. This forwarding logic passes the value produced in the output of the EX stage back to the input of the EX stage directly without going through the registers, as shown in Figure 6.5. *Short-circuiting* the registers in this way allows the value produced by one instruction to be available as the input to a following instruction much more quickly than if the value first had to be written to a register.

All of these techniques are discussed more completely in the next chapter where we describe how to implement a five-stage pipeline for the VeSPA ISA.

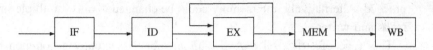

Figure 6.5. When a RAW hazard is detected between two instructions, *forwarding* logic in a pipeline can be used to bypass the register write operation by passing the value produced in the EX stage by the first instruction back to the input of the EX stage for use by the following dependent instruction. The register write eventually is performed when the instruction reaches the WB stage so that the value continues to be available for any later instructions that need it.

6.5 Summary

Pipelining is a processor design technique used to speed up the execution of programs. Pipelining does not reduce the amount of time required to execute any single instruction. Rather, it allows multiple instructions to be in various stages of their execution simultaneously. In the ideal case, a new instruction can complete every cycle resulting in an ideal speedup equal to the number of stages in the pipeline, compared to an implementation that is not pipelined. However, we seldom achieve this ideal speedup due to program dependences. These dependences lead to pipeline hazards, which force the processor to insert bubbles into the pipeline, or require the designer to add logic to pass values between intermediate pipeline stages. In the next chapter, we will learn how to use Verilog to implement a pipelined version of the VeSPA processor.

Further reading

The following books provide a comprehensive discussion of the issues involved in pipelining a processor.

H. G. Cragon, *Computer Architecture and Implementation*. Cambridge, UK: Cambridge University Press, 2000.

V. P. Heuring and H. F. Jordan, *Computer Systems Design and Architecture*, (2nd edn.) Prentice Hall, 2003.

D. Patterson and J. Hennessy, *Computer Organization and Design: The Hardware/Software Interface, 2nd edn*. Morgan Kaufmann, 1997.

7 Implementation of the pipelined processor

The problem is not that there are problems. The problem is expecting otherwise and thinking that having problems is a problem.

Theodore Rubin

7.1 Pipelining VeSPA

An overview of the structure of a pipelined processor was provided in the previous chapter. We will now fill in the details and add flesh to the skeletal concepts introduced earlier, at the end of which we will have developed a block-level structure for the processor that can be implemented in Verilog. Our processor will consist of the following five pipelined stages, the instruction fetch (IF) stage, the instruction decode (ID) stage, the execute (EX) stage, the memory (MEM) stage, and the write back (WB) stage. We will interchangeably refer to these as the first through the fifth stages, respectively.

Such an instruction pipeline may be defined at the behavioral level or the structural level. At the behavioral level, the hardware may be modeled as a finite state machine that performs IF in the first stage, ID in the second, and so on, with Moore outputs generated in each stage, corresponding to the control signals that are used to activate the instructions. An example of such a description is provided for a simple processor in a book on VHDL-based design by Roth (see the Further reading section at the end of this chapter).

Instead of such an approach, we choose to describe the circuit at the structural level in this chapter, in order to get the reader 'closer to the hardware'. This structural description shows interconnections between blocks such as ALUs, MUXs and registers, as well as more fundamental gates. To avoid entanglement in cumbersome notation, we do not specifically show the Verilog implementation here, although a processor model in Verilog is available on the companion web site. The top level module instantiates the hazard detection unit and the five stages of the pipeline, in addition to some global constructs such as the register file, the memory and the clock generator. We now describe the specifics of each of the major modules in the hardware.

7.2 The hazard detection unit

A hazard detection unit is designed to check for potential hazards, and to determine when the pipeline is to be stalled, when bubbles are to be introduced, and when data must be forwarded in each stage of the pipeline. Each stage of the pipeline consists of several MUXs, and the hazard detection unit generates the control inputs for these MUXs. We will overview these signals here, and for simplicity, in our subsequent discussion of various pipeline stages in Section 7.4, we will not list these control inputs in detail.

As described in the previous chapter, the use of an instruction pipeline implies that one must allow for and design around three classes of hazards: branch hazards, data hazards, and structural hazards. By construction, we ensure that structural hazards are not an issue, and therefore we ignore them in this section.

Branch hazards may be detected once the instruction enters the ID stage of the pipeline; if the branch is taken, then the pipeline must be flushed by inserting pipeline bubbles (i.e., NOP instructions). Therefore, these hazards are relatively easy to capture by incorporating circuitry in the second stage that determines whether the branch condition is satisfied or not, and feeding this to the hazard detection unit that generates appropriate control signals that control MUXs that allow for the possibility of flushing the pipeline using NOPs when the specified set of branch conditions is satisfied.

Due to the structure of the pipeline, data hazards cannot manifest themselves as WAR or WAW hazards, but allowances must be made to prevent RAW hazards. During the normal operation of the pipeline, the register writes occur at the end of the fifth stage (i.e., on the sixth clock), while register reads take place in the second stage, reading the contents of the register as established at the second clock cycle. As a consequence, an instruction that requires a register read immediately after a register write can lead to a RAW hazard, implying that early stages of the pipeline must be stalled and NOPs inserted.

Therefore, structurally, the pipeline must be modified to permit the insertion of pipeline bubbles to handle flushing and stalling. The performance of the pipeline can be improved by the use of forwarding, whereby the number of NOPs to be introduced in the pipeline is minimized. The hazard detection unit generates the control signals that enable the MUXs in the instruction pipeline to perform the appropriate function at each step.

Hazard detection may be achieved by examining the instruction set and determining:

1. the earliest pipeline stage at which the results of an instruction are available; and
2. the latest stage at which the contents of a register are used in the pipeline.

Using this information, instead of waiting for the register write in the sixth clock cycle, the instruction stream in the pipeline may be examined so that data can be forwarded to the next instruction immediately when the results are available, instead of waiting for the sixth clock cycle. Meanwhile, the next instruction may continue execution up to the stage at which the results are needed, which is often later than the second stage.

Table 7.1 shows the RAW dependences between various classes of instructions. For the various classes of instructions listed in the first row, the earliest pipeline stage at which the results of the instruction are available are shown in parentheses. For example, for ALU instructions, the results are available after four clock cycles. Note that within the entire instruction set, the only instructions that must be considered here are the ALU instructions, LD, LDI, LDX, and JMPL. It is easily verified that the remaining instructions (NOP, Bxx, JMP, ST, STX and HLT) do not write to a register and hence cannot create a RAW dependence. For the STX instruction in particular, two register reads are required: the rs1 register can be read as late as the third clock cycle, while rst can be read as late as the fourth clock cycle.

The latest pipeline stage at which the contents of a register are utilized are shown in the first column of the table. Here again, the instructions are divided into classes, and only those instructions that require a register read are considered.

If an instruction I_1 is followed by instruction I_2, then the difference between the earliest write time of I_1 and the latest read time of I_2 is shown in the cell in Table 7.1

Table 7.1. *An analysis of the RAW dependences in the pipeline for operations that perform read and write operations on the register file. The numbers in parentheses in row 1 represent the earliest time when the results of the corresponding instruction in row 1 are available, and the those in column 1 show the latest read time for the instructions.*

Instruction Class	ALU (4)	LD/LDX (5)	LDI (3)	JMPL (2)
ALU (3)	1	2	0	−1
LDX (3)	1	2	0	−1
ST (4)	0	1	−1	−2
STX (rs1) (3)	1	2	0	−1
STX (rst) (4)	0	1	−1	−2
JMP/JMPL (3)	1	2	0	−1
Bxx (2)	2	N/A	N/A	N/A

that corresponds to (I_1, I_2). Since I_2 lags I_1 by one stage in normal operation, if this number is less than or equal to 1, the RAW dependence can be removed by the use of forwarding. In the cases where this number exceeds 1 (shown in boldface), pipeline forwarding alone is insufficient, and it is essential to insert pipeline bubbles.

An example of forwarding can be shown for the case where I_1 and I_2 are both ALU instructions. A quick glance at the table shows that a difference of one cycle is permissible, provided the data can be forwarded from the result of I_1 at the end of stage 3 (i.e., at the fourth clock cycle for I_1) to I_2 at the beginning of stage 3 (namely, at the end of the third clock cycle for I_2).

Note that since a branch instruction Bxx is conditional on the C, N, V or Z flag, and is therefore only dependent on an ALU operation, the remaining entries in the row of Bxx are not applicable. In case an ALU operation precedes a Bxx instruction, the flags are set at the end of the fourth stage, while the branch decision must be made in the second stage. Consequently, the pipeline may be stalled and bubbles introduced until such time as the flags from stage 4 may be forwarded to stage 2.

Another example where a pipeline bubble must be inserted is the case when I_1 is an LD/LDX instruction and I_2 is an ALU instruction; note that in this case, the corresponding entry in the table is 2. The ALU instruction requires the data in stage 3, but the LD/LDX can only provide it in stage 5. This dependence can be detected when the ALU instruction enters the ID stage, and at this time, the pipeline is stalled for one cycle by inserting a single bubble to create the requisite time gap that then permits the correct data from the LD/LDX instruction to be forwarded from stage 5 to stage 3, in time for the ALU computation.

7.3 Overview of the pipeline structure

Figure 7.1 illustrates the five stages of the pipeline, the intermediate registers, and the forwarded data. Notationally, the numeral at the end of each register indicates the stage number of the pipeline that it feeds. The IF stage propagates the instruction and program counter to the ID stage through the IR2 and PC2 registers, respectively.

From the ID stage to the EX stage, a larger number of intermediate registers is introduced. As before, we propagate the instruction and program counter, this time through IR3 and PC3. As we will see later, this includes mechanisms to handle pipeline stalls and bubbles. Notably, any pipeline stalls are performed at this stage. In addition, we also propagate

- a condition bit that is set to one if the instruction in the ID stage is a branch instruction, and if the branch condition holds;
- the X3 and Y3 registers that feed the ALU inputs; and
- an MD3 register that carries data to be written to the memory.

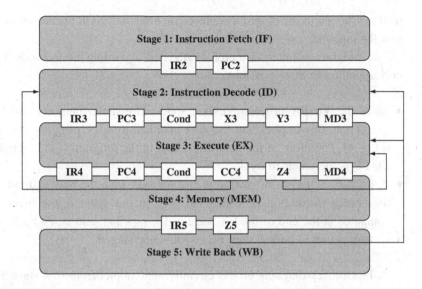

Figure 7.1. An overview of the structure of the pipeline, showing the stages, registers, and forwarded signals.

During memory write instructions, the ALU inputs may be used for address computation, and hence the data to be written is stored in the MD3 register.

The EX stage propagates the condition bit from the ID stage, and also has an IR4 and PC4 for the instruction register and the program counter, respectively. As before, these may be configured for introducing pipeline bubbles, but configuration for pipeline stalls is not necessary since these are processed in the ID stage. Besides these registers, the memory write data is stored in the MD4 register, the ALU results are stored in the Z4 register, and the condition codes in the CC4 register. Finally, the MEM stage only propagates the instruction register to IR5, and the register write data to the Z5 register.

As shown in the figure, data forwarding is implemented by feeding back the Z4, Z5 and CC4 bits to various pipeline stages.

7.4   A detailed description of the pipeline stages

7.4.1   The instruction fetch (IF) stage

The address of the current instruction is stored in the program counter (PC). During normal operation, the instruction fetch stage addresses the instruction memory using the program counter, so that the current instruction may be brought in and loaded into the instruction register (IR). The program counter is then updated to point to the next instruction to be introduced into the pipeline. When the pipeline is stalled, the next instruction in the program is placed on hold, and NOP operations are introduced into the pipeline.

The program counter is therefore updated according to the following scheme, corresponding to three possible states:

- Since the VeSPA processor uses a byte-addressable memory, and has a 32-bit instruction, this implies that the next instruction in the program is at the location $(PC + 4)$. Therefore, if the next instruction in the program is to be brought into the IR, PC is incremented by 4.
- If, instead, a branch instruction is encountered, then the new address specified by the branch instruction is loaded into PC. In our scheme, the branch address is computed at the end of the EX stage of the pipeline, and is fed back from there.
- If the pipeline is stalled, then PC remains unchanged.

A block-level diagram of the circuitry that implements this stage is shown in Figure 7.2. The PC is updated through a MUX, according to the conditions listed above.

The IF stage communicates with the ID stage by updating the IR2 and PC2 registers, respectively. The former is updated by a MUX that passes through either the instruction from the instruction memory, or a NOP, or recirculates the current value of IR2 in case of a pipeline stall. The latter is updated through another MUX

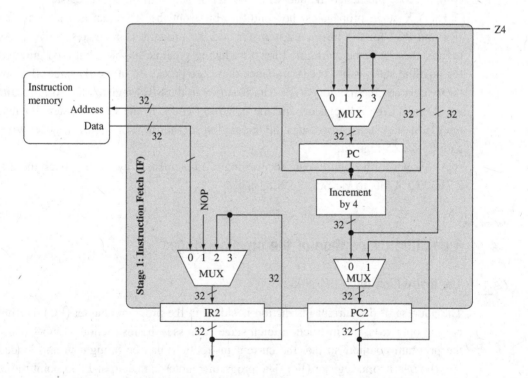

Figure 7.2. The IF stage of the instruction pipeline.

that passes either PC+4 or retains the current value of PC2, depending on whether the pipeline is to be stalled or not.

7.4.2 The instruction decode (ID) stage

In stage 2, shown in Figure 7.3, the contents of the instruction register and the program counter are passed on to stage 3 through the IR3 and PC3 registers, respectively. The value of IR3 is chosen by a MUX to be either the value of IR2, a NOP instruction (in case of a pipeline flush), or a recirculation of the present value of IR3 (in case of a stall). The contents of PC3 are either taken from PC2 or by recirculating the current value (in case of a pipeline stall).

The second stage of the pipeline decodes the instruction in the IR2 register. Recall that the first five bits of the instruction store the opcode, and for various types of instructions, the following schemes are used:

- For arithmetic and logical instructions (ADD, SUB, OR, AND, NOT, XOR, and CMP), the operands are specified as the addresses of the source register(s) and the destination register when the immediate bit (bit 16) is zero.

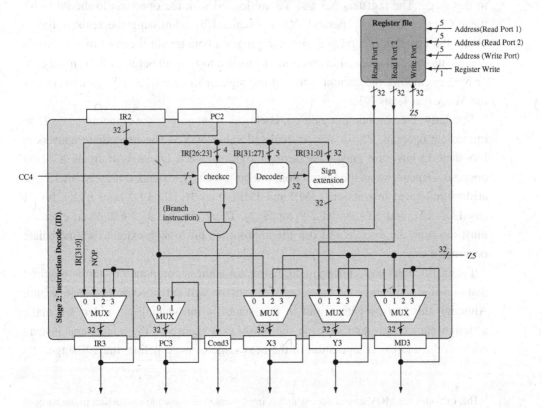

Figure 7.3. The ID stage of the instruction pipeline.

- For control instructions, a condition code is tested based on bits 26 through 23 of the instruction word, and a destination address is specified either as an immediate address for a branch instruction (Bxx), or as an immediate address with an offset stored in a register for a jump instruction (JMP, JMPL). JMPL differs from JMP in that bit 16 is one, and that its execution requires the PC to be stored in a register before executing the jump.
- For data transfer instructions[1], an immediate address (LD) or data value (LDI) is specified. The indexed load instruction (LDX) also specifies a register offset. The store instructions ST and STX are similar in nature to LD and LDX, respectively, except that the data is stored instead of loaded into memory.

For branch instructions, along with the opcode, the carry (C), zero (Z), negative (N) and overflow (V) flags from the ALU are fed into a condition code checker to determine whether a branch is to be taken or not. The output of this checker circuit goes to the condition bit flip-flop at the interface of the second and third stages.

A triple-ported register file that permits two simultaneous reads along with a write operation is used in order to remove the possibility of register file access dependences in this stage. The registers X3 and Y3 are loaded with the operands to the ALU for the EX stage. The first operand, X3, is obtained by addressing the register file to obtain the contents of `rs1`, or from the program counter (in the case of an address computation for an indexed instruction), or from a forwarded output, Z5, from stage 5, or by recirculating the current status of the register in case of a stall, as depicted by the MUX that feeds X3.

Similarly, the second operand, Y3, is chosen from among the contents of `rs2`, an immediate operand, Z5, or the recirculated value of Y3. The immediate address is less than 32 bits, and must pass through sign-extension circuitry to create a 32-bit operand. Depending on the instruction, the bit to be sign-extended may be bit 15 (for arithmetic/logical instructions, JMP and JMPL), bit 16 (for LDX and STX), bit 21 (for LDI, LD, and ST), or bit 22 (for Bxx). Therefore, the sign-extension circuitry must examine the opcode and use the appropriate bit to sign-extend the immediate operand, if any.

For instructions with indexed addressing, an address computation step is required that sums the contents of the index register with the sign-extended immediate operand. Although this can be carried out in this stage by introducing an adder, we make a design choice here and save on the hardware expense of the adder, and instead perform the address computation in the next stage of the pipeline, the EX stage.

---

[1] This excludes the MOV instruction, which is implemented as a pseudo-instruction in the form of an ADD.

Finally, for store instructions, the operand to be stored is placed in the MD3 register. The MUX input to MD3 selects one of `rs2` or Z5 in normal operation; additionally, in case of a pipeline stall, the value of MD3 is retained.

7.4.3   The execute (EX) stage

The EX stage performs any arithmetic and logical computations that are necessary, and sets the condition code bits appropriately. The structure of this stage is shown in Figure 7.4.

As before, the contents of the IR and PC and transmitted to the next stage, this time through the IR4 and PC4 registers. The IR4 register may be fed by either the IR3 register, or with a NOP in case the pipeline is to be flushed, while the PC4 register simply transmits the contents of PC3. As mentioned earlier, all stalls are handled in stage 2 of the pipeline, so that in this stage, the MUX inputs to the registers that transmit the values to stage 5 do not have recirculating inputs.

The ALU outputs are transmitted to the next stage through the Z4 register; in addition, this output goes to a condition flag generating circuit that transmits the condition codes (C, Z, N and V) to the next stage through the CC register. The inputs to the ALU, X and Y, are selected by a pair of MUXs. The MUX input to X may

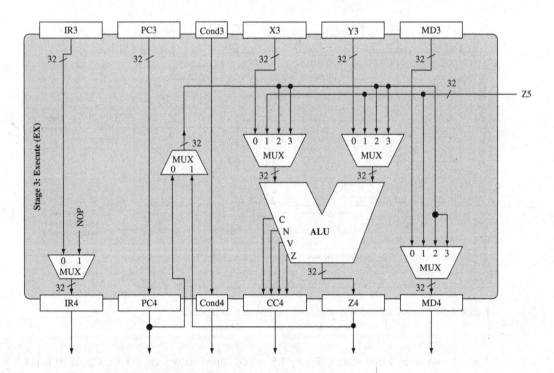

Figure 7.4. The EX stage of the instruction pipeline.

choose either X3, the forwarded operand Z5, PC4 or Z4. The MUX input to Y is similar, except that Y3 is used instead of X3.

All addresses for memory accesses are provided by the Z4 register. In case of address computations for indexed instructions, this is natural since the ALU is used to perform these computations. For instructions where an immediate address is provided, the ALU simply passes the immediate instruction directly from Y3 to Z4.

Finally, the condition bit is transmitted to the next stage, and MD4 (for memory access instructions) is selected from one among MD3, Z5, PC4 and Z4[2].

7.4.4 The memory access (MEM) and write back (WB) stages

The last two stages are illustrated in Figure 7.5. The MEM stage performs that task of performing read/write operations from and to the memory. Therefore, the primary task performed here is that of transmitting a memory address, and sending or receiving the data to be written or read.

For memory accesses, the address is taken from the Z4 register, and read (RD) and write (WR) signals are generated and sent to memory: if RD is one, then the memory access is a read, and if WR is one, then the access is a write. If both signals are zero, no memory transactions take place in this stage. The data to be written may either be taken from the MD4 register, or from the Z5 register (in case of data forwarding).

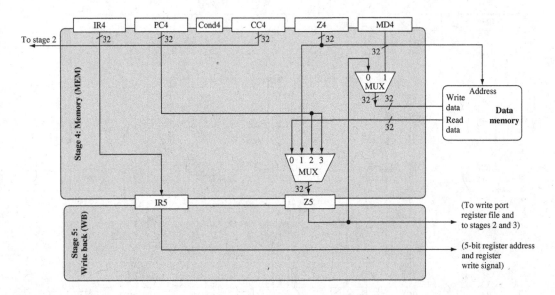

Figure 7.5. The MEM and WB stages of the instruction pipeline.

---

[2] As we look at the MEM stage in Figure 7.5, it may superficially seem that the Cond4 bit is not connected anywhere. This is, in fact, not true; this bit is used by the hazard detection unit.

The data read from memory goes into the Z5 register. Note that since Z5 is used as a forwarding register, it may also take other inputs in case the instruction that is being executed does not involve a memory read or write. Specifically, an input MUX into Z5 chooses one among the data from memory, the contents of PC4, and the contents of Z4.

The final stage executes any writes that must be performed in the register file. Specifically, if the destination in an instruction is a register, then a register address and data are sent to the register file, along with a write signal.

7.5   Timing considerations

As we discussed previously in Section 6.2, one of the primary goals of pipelining is to increase the performance of the processor. Pipelining achieves this goal primarily by executing several instructions in parallel. Another advantage provided by pipelining, though, is that it allows the designer to use a faster clock frequency than could be used in an equivalent nonpipelined design.

The minimum clock period required in a pipelined processor is determined by the signal propagation delays through each stage of the pipeline. That is, the clock period must be long enough to allow every signal in each stage to propagate from the pipeline registers at the input to a stage to the pipeline registers at the output of a stage. In the ID stage shown in Figure 7.3, for instance, signals must propagate from register IR2 through several levels of logic to IR3, Cond3, Y3, and so on. Similarly, signals from the register file also must propagate through several levels of logic to the corresponding pipeline registers that form the frontier between pipeline stages 2 and 3.

At least one propagation path from the input pipeline registers to the output pipeline registers in a stage will be the longest path for that stage. This longest path is called the *critical path* for that stage. The longest of these critical path delays from each pipeline stage will determine the minimum clock period for the entire pipeline since all of the registers in all of the pipeline stages are synchronously clocked with the same clock. This longest path is called the processor's critical path delay.

To achieve the highest performance, the designer needs to minimize the processor's critical path delay. This goal is realized by balancing the number of levels of logic between the input and output pipeline registers for each pipeline stage. That is, the smallest clock period is usually obtained when the critical path delays in each pipeline stage are approximately equal. Balancing the path delays in this way is determined by the partitioning of the operations required for the *fetch-execute* cycle into individual pipeline stages.

Of particular concern when using the stage partitioning described in Section 6.1 is the delay in the ID and MEM stages. The problem is that the time required to access memory to read an instruction, or to read or write a data value, is substantially longer than the time required to propagate a signal through the logic of the other pipeline stages. If we chose a clock period that allowed a memory access to occur in one cycle, we would end up with an extremely slow processor.

To get around this problem of very slow memories, we typically introduce instruction and data *caches*. An *instruction cache*, or *i-cache*, is a small memory that temporarily stores instructions that have recently been referenced by the processor. When an instruction is fetched in the IF stage, the processor logic will first look to see if the desired word from memory, that is, a word with the address currently been referenced, has already been loaded into the i-cache. If it has, we say that the memory reference has *hit* in the cache. The instruction stored at that address then can be moved into the IF stage.

If the desired address is not in the cache, however, we say that the memory reference *misses* in the cache. In this case, the processor logic must read the word from the main memory and move it into the cache. After the word is in the cache, it can be moved into the IF stage. Since the memory is much slower than the processor pipeline, the logic that services the cache miss must freeze the pipeline until the instruction has been read from memory and moved into the cache.

A separate data cache, or *d-cache*, can be used to store data values in a similar manner so that the MEM stage does not have to wait for an entire memory read or write operation.

The time required to access any memory structure, such as a cache or a register file, is proportional to its size. That is, a large memory structure requires more time to access than a small structure. So that the i- and d-caches can be accessed in a single cycle, they must be made relatively small compared to the size of the main memory. By carefully adjusting the size of the cache, the designer can make its access time match the speed required by the IF and MEM pipeline stages.

It is possible to increase the number of pipeline stages to help match the pipeline's clock frequency to the cache access time. The MEM pipeline stage, for example, could be spread across two separate stages to allow it to access a cache that is slower than a single cycle. In this case, a memory read operation would send the address to the cache in the first MEM stage. The value then would be read from the cache in a new, second MEM stage.

Increasing the number of pipeline stages reduces the number of levels of logic in each stage. Fewer levels of logic then allow for a faster clock. In addition, more instructions will execute simultaneously as the number of pipeline stages is increased. On the other hand, each additional pipeline stage will add one more cycle to the execution time of each instruction. Furthermore, additional pipeline stages will increase the branch penalty by forcing more bubbles into the pipeline when a branch is *taken*. Similarly, more bubbles will be need to be inserted in the pipeline to tolerate other types of hazards. One of the challenges in designing a pipelined processor is to find the right balance between the number of pipeline stages and the resulting clock period. Cragon (see Further Reading at the end of this chapter) discusses this trade-off in more detail, and suggests a way of finding an optimal balance.

7.6   Summary

This chapter has demonstrated the implementation of the instruction pipeline, showing how the design must choose intermediate registers and forwarded signals, and displaying the innards of each of the pipeline stages. During our exposition, we have made several design choices that impact, positively or negatively, the performance of the pipeline. For instance, the use of forwarding adds hardware overhead but potentially provides significant speedups. The reader is invited to investigate other design tradeoffs that can result in a hardware/performance tradeoff.

Further reading

H. G. Cragon, *Computer Architecture and Implementation.* Cambridge, UK: Cambridge University Press, 2000. *See Section 6.2, in particular.*

C. H. Roth, Jr., *Digital Systems Design using VHDL.* Boston, MA: PWS Publishing Company, 1998. *See Chapter 11 in particular.*

8 Verification

Aristotle maintained that women have fewer teeth than men; although he was twice married, it never occurred to him to verify this statement by examining his wives' mouths.

Bertrand Russell, (1872–1970).

A processor design cannot be considered complete until it has undergone a rigorous verification process. The goal of this verification process is to ensure that the processor behaves as specified in the ISA under all possible conditions and all possible input combinations. Of course, due to the number of potential inputs and states, this is an impossible goal. Instead, we try to verify each component of the processor as rigorously as possible within the given time and resource constraints. We also try to verify the operation of the entire processor after all of the components have been assembled into a complete system.

In this chapter, we first look at using Verilog *test benches* to verify the operation of individual processor modules. We examine two types of test bench. The first, which we call *directed testing*, uses inputs that are carefully chosen to exercise specific aspects of the module being tested. The second type of testing uses pseudorandom inputs to automatically exercise a very large number of input combinations.

After learning about these module-level testing techniques, we introduce the idea of *self-test* programs. These tests are written in the processor's assembly language, or in a high-level programming language that is compiled into the processor's assembly language. When the self-test program is executed, it verifies that the different operations it performs are actually being executed correctly. This testing technique is particularly useful for verifying the operation of the entire processor as each individual instruction is executed.

8.1 Component-level test benches

A *test bench* is a program written in Verilog that is used to stimulate the inputs of a Verilog hardware module and compare the outputs produced to the values expected. Test benches are an important technique for semi-automatically verifying the proper operation of a component.

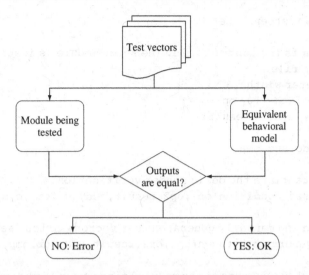

Figure 8.1. A test bench requires additional Verilog code to read or generate the test vectors; to drive these test vectors as inputs to both the module being tested and the behavioral module; and, finally, to compare the outputs of the module being tested with the outputs of the behavioral module.

As shown in Figure 8.1, the testing process begins with a set of test vectors. These test vectors can be produced either manually by the system designer, or they can be generated automatically using some sort of pseudorandom test vector generation. The test vectors then are applied as the inputs to the Verilog module being tested. This module is simulated and its output values are examined.

We could check the outputs manually to verify that they are the results that we expect for the given inputs. However, it is much more efficient if we can automate this process. The trick to automating this checking process is to somehow automatically determine what the outputs *should be* when the given inputs are applied.

Fortunately, as we have seen previously, Verilog provides us with very powerful behavioral modeling capabilities. Thus, we can write a simple behavioral model that provides the same functionality as the hardware module we are testing. The test bench then applies the same test vector as the inputs to both the module being tested and to the behavioral model. The outputs of both modules are compared by the checker module. If the two sets of outputs do not match, an error is reported. If they do match, though, then the module being tested must be producing the correct output for that test vector. (This assumes, of course, that the behavioral model produces the correct output.) The next test vector then is applied and the entire process is repeated until we have no more test vectors.

8.1.1   Using manually generated test vectors

Manually generating test vectors is perhaps the most straightforward way of testing a hardware module. The idea is to provide inputs to the module that will force it

```
module testbench_setcc;

// This is the top most file. The setcc module is instantiated within
// this file.
parameter width = 32;
wire [width-1:0] op1,op2;
wire [width:0] result;

wire add,sub,cmp;

// Instantiate the design under verification.
setcc set_condition(op1,op2,result,add,sub,cmp,c,z,n,v);

// Read the manually generated test vectors to test setcc.
data_generator datagen(op1,op2,result,add,sub,cmp,clk);

// Check the outputs of the module being tested with the expected outputs.
checker check(op1,op2,result,add,sub,cmp,c,z,n,v,clk);

// Instantiate Oscillator
oscillator osc(clk,clk_n);

endmodule
```

Figure 8.2.   A Verilog test bench used to read manually generated test vectors from a file and apply them to the setcc module.

to respond to all of the most basic logical combinations and *corner cases*[1]. The Verilog code in Figure 8.2 shows how to implement a straightforward test bench using manually generated test vectors for verifying the setcc logic for VeSPA (see Section 4.6 for a description of this portion of the processor).

The data_generator module instantiated in this test bench, shown in Figure 8.3, reads the test vectors from the input file. It also produces the expected output for the module using the behavioral arithmetic operations. As read by the $fopen statement in this module, the input test vectors are stored in a plain text file called test_vectors. The $fscanf statement in this module reads each

[1] *Corner cases* are those situations or input combinations that typically do not occur often in an executing system. For instance, a corner case may be what happens when a system is executing at its extreme limits along some dimension. Corner cases are important to carefully verify, however, since they often represent the most complex or unusual combinations of events and inputs. Checking the corner cases can very often expose design or implementation errors that can affect the more common operations.

```
module data_generator(op1,op2,result,add,sub,cmp,clk);

parameter width = 32;
output [width-1:0] op1,op2;
output [width:0] result;
output add,sub,cmp;
input clk;

integer input_file;
integer EOF;
reg [width-1:0] op1,op2;
reg [width:0] result;
reg add,sub,cmp;

initial
  begin
  input_file = $fopen("./test_vectors","r");
  if (input_file == 0)
    $stop;
  end

always @(posedge clk)
  begin
    #(5);
    EOF = $fscanf(input_file, "%h %h %b %b %b",op1,op2,add, sub,cmp);
    if(EOF == -1)
      $stop;
    if(add == 1)
      result = op1 + op2;
    else
      result = op1 - op2;
  end
endmodule
```

Figure 8.3. This module is used in the test bench of Figure 8.2 to read the test vectors and generate the expected output.

test vector from this file. The variable EOF is set to -1 when all of the test vectors in the file have been read. The input specification in the $fscanf statement shows that the test vector should consist of two hex numbers that represent two input operands, followed by three binary values. These three binary values, add, sub, cmp, are inputs to the setcc module that indicate what arithmetic operation has been performed.

Figure 8.4 shows several example test vectors that would be used to drive this test bench. Each line corresponds to a separate input vector. The first two values of each vector are the 32-bit input operand values. The remaining three binary values

ffffffff	ffffffff	1	0	0
00000000	00000000	0	0	1
11111111	11111111	0	1	0
00000000	ffffffff	1	0	0
00000000	ffffffff	0	1	0
7fffffff	7fffffff	1	0	0
10000000	10000000	0	1	0
10000000	10000000	0	0	1

Figure 8.4. Example test vectors used by the module in Figure 8.3.

indicate the specific operation that is being performed by the ALU. Only one of these three binary values should be asserted within a test vector, as defined in the VeSPA ISA. The first test vector indicates that operation being tested is $(-1) + (-1)$, for instance.

The Verilog definition of the checker module instantiated in Figure 8.2 is shown in Figure 8.5. This module takes as inputs the condition bits generated by the module being tested, setcc. These inputs are the variables c, z, n, and v. It also takes as inputs the test vector values and the corresponding result passed from the data_generator module, that is, op1, op2, result, add, sub, and cmp. It then uses behavioral statements to generate the values that are expected to be produced by setcc. These expected values are assigned to the variables ref_c, ref_v, ref_n, and ref_z. Finally, these expected values are compared to the values actually produced by the module being tested using the if statement. If there is a mismatch, an error is reported and the testing is allowed to continue.

The number of test vectors that are manually generated by the designer will determine how long this test bench will run. Obviously, the more test vectors generated, the more thoroughly the module will be tested. The test vectors shown in Figure 8.4 provide only enough inputs to verify the most basic operation of the setcc module. A more complete verification will require substantially more input vectors. The question, though, is how these additional vectors should be generated.

8.1.2   Using automatically generated test vectors

Manually generated test vectors are very useful for verifying the basic operation of a module, and for forcing unusual conditions (i.e., corner cases). The primary limitation of manually generated test vectors, however, is the difficulty of generating them. It simply is not feasible to generate enough test vectors manually to cover all of the possible input combinations for the module being tested. For instance, the input test vectors for the example in the previous section each require two 32-bit input operands and three binary values. Completely verifying all possible input combinations for this simple module would require $2^{32} \times 2^{32}$ values to cover all of the input operand possibilities. These combinations would have to be repeated for each of the three

```
module checker(op1,op2,result,add,sub,cmp,c,z,n,v,clk);

parameter width = 32;
input add,sub,cmp,clk,c,z,n,v;
input [width-1:0] op1,op2;
input [width:0] result;

reg ref_c,ref_v,ref_n,ref_z,subt;

initial
  begin
    $display("OPERAND1\tOPERAND2\tRESULT  ADD  SUB  CMP");
    $display("===========================================");
  end

always @(posedge clk)
  begin
    #(20);
    $display("%h\t%h\t%h  %b  %b  %b  at time %d",op1,op2, result,
             add,sub,cmp,$time);
    subt  = sub || cmp ;
    ref_c = result[width];
    ref_z = ~(|result[width-1:0]);
    ref_n = result[width-1];
    ref_v = ( result[width-1] & ~ op1[width-1] & ~(subt ^op2 [width-1]))
          | (~result[width-1] & op1[width-1] & (subt ^op2 [width-1]));

  if( (ref_c != c) || (ref_z != z) || (ref_n != n) || (ref_v !=v) )
  begin
    $display("-E- Error in verifying condition codes");
    $display("Computed CC: C = %b Z = %b N = %b V = %b",c,z,n,v);
    $display("Reference CC: C = %b Z = %b N = %b V = %b",ref_c,
             ref_z,ref_n,ref_v);
    $stop;
  end
  else
    $display("Condition codes verified C = %b Z = %b N = %b V = %b",c,z,n,v);
  end
endmodule
```

Figure 8.5. This module compares the actual values produced by the module being tested with the expected values.

possible combinations of the single-bit inputs for a total of $3 \times 2^{32} \times 2^{32} = 3 \times 2^{64}$ unique test vectors. It would require nearly two million years to test all of these input combinations if each test vector could be simulated in only 1 microsecond. Obviously, it is not feasible to exhaustively test even this simple circuit.

Instead of testing every possible input combination, we can randomly generate a very large number of test vectors automatically using Verilog's pseudorandom number generator. This random number generator allows us to cover a wide range of values to uncover potential errors without having to generate all possible input combinations. Pseudorandom testing also can sometimes generate test vectors for combinations that a person may not even think of.

Figure 8.6 shows how the basic test bench from Figure 8.2 is modified to perform this type of pseudorandom testing. In fact, all that needs to be changed is to replace the `data_generator` module with the `random_data_generator` module.

The `random_data_generator` module is shown in Figure 8.7. Instead of reading the test vectors from a file, as was done in Figure 8.2, this module randomly generates operand values using the `$random` function. The number of random vectors generated is controlled by the `if($time > 100000)` statement. Increasing the 100 000 time unit limit will allow more test vectors to be generated. Other than using a different technique for generating test vectors, the remainder of the test process is the same as that described in the previous section.

```
module testbench_setcc;

// This is the top most file. The setcc module is instantiated within
// this file.
parameter width = 32;
wire [width-1:0] op1,op2;
wire [width:0] result;

wire add,sub,cmp;

// Instantiate the design under verification
setcc set_condition(op1,op2,result,add,sub,cmp,c,z,n,v);

// Read the manually generated test vectors to test setcc.
random_data_generator datagen(op1,op2,result,add,sub,cmp,clk);

// Check the outputs of the module being tested with the expected outputs
checker check(op1,op2,result,add,sub,cmp,c,z,n,v,clk);

// Instantiate Oscillator
oscillator osc(clk,clk_n);

endmodule
```

Figure 8.6. A Verilog test bench that uses automatically generated test vectors for verifying the setcc module.

```verilog
module random_data_generator(op1,op2,result,add,sub,cmp,clk);

parameter width = 32;
output [width-1:0] op1,op2;
output [width:0] result;
output add,sub,cmp;
input clk;

integer input_file;
integer i;
reg [width-1:0] op1,op2;
reg [width:0] result;
reg add,sub,cmp;

always @(posedge clk)
  begin
    #(5);
    if($time > 100000)
        $stop;
    op1 = $random;
    op2 = $random;
    add = $random;
    if (add == 1 )
        begin
          sub = 0;
          cmp = 0;
          result = op1 + op2;
        end
  else
        begin
          sub = $random;
          if (sub == 1)
              cmp = 0;
          else
              cmp = 1;
          result = op1 - op2;
        end
  end
 endmodule
```

Figure 8.7. This module generates pseudorandom test vectors for verifying the setcc module.

8.1.3 Constrained pseudorandom test vectors

The pseudorandom test vector generation shown in Figure 8.7 allows all possible input combinations to be generated. In some situations, though, not all of the input combinations are valid. For instance, when testing the VeSPA ALU, not all of the possible opcode values are valid ALU opcodes. In this type of situation, each test vector must be compared to the range of valid inputs as it is generated. Any generated vector that is outside of the range of valid inputs must be thrown away and a new vector generated to replace it. This type of test vector generation is called *constrained pseudorandom test vector generation.* An example of how these constraints can be applied is shown in Figure 8.8 for testing the VeSPA ALU.

```
module rnd_data_generator(opcode,alu_x,alu_y,clk);

parameter width = 32;

output [4:0] opcode;
output [width-1:0] alu_x,alu_y;
input clk;

integer i;
integer seed_op,seed_x,seed_y;
reg [4:0] opcode;
reg [width-1:0] alu_x,alu_y;

initial
  begin
  i = 0;
  $display("OPCODE(dec)\ t\ t\ tALU_X(hex)\ t\ t\ tALU_Y(hex)\ t\ t\ t
          TIME");
  $display("===============================================");
  end
always @(posedge clk)
  begin
    #(5);
    opcode = $random;
  // Constrain the opcodes to be an ALU operation
  // such that 0 <= opcode <= 13
    while ((opcode > 14) && (opcode < 31))
    opcode = $random;
    alu_x = $random;
    alu_y = $random;
    $display("-I-%d\ t\ t\ t%h\ t\ t\ t%h\ t%d", opcode,alu_x,alu_y,
            $time);
    i = i+1;
    // if (i == 17)
    //   $stop;
  end
endmodule
```

Figure 8.8. This module generates pseudorandom test vectors for the VeSPA ALU where the possible opcodes that are generated are constrained to be only valid opcodes.

Several test benches for the VeSPA processor design are available on the companion web site. These include both manually generated test vectors, plus pseudorandom test vectors.

8.1.4   Initialization

When doing this type of testbench testing, it is important to recall that a sequential circuit may begin in an arbitrary initial state that is a random function of how it is powered up. To remove this unpredictability during verification, the hardware may be designed in such a way that all memory elements can be reset to logic 0 (it is also possible to set them to logic 1, but logic 0 is a more conventional choice). This drives the finite state machine representing the system to a *reset* state. If, during testing, it is necessary to drive the data in the memory elements to specific logic values, an appropriate set of state transitions may be selected from the state diagram to drive the state machine to the corresponding state.

For instance, in the previous example in Figure 2.4, resetting all flip-flops would take the state machine to S0. If the objective is to set the flip-flops corresponding to the lower two state bits to logic 1, this may be achieved by driving the system to state S3 in three cycles, setting `adventure` $= 1$ in the first, `sword_sharpened` $= 1$ in the second, and `courage` $=$ `dragon` $= 1$ in the third.

8.2   System-level self-testing

Due to the complexity of generating test vectors for a complete processor, test benches are typically used to verify only the components within an overall system. A complementary approach for verifying the correct operation of an entire digital system, such as the VeSPA processor, is to write *self-test* programs in the processor's assembly language, or in some high-level programming language. These test programs are written, compiled, and assembled on some existing computer system. The resulting object code then is executed on the processor being tested.

If written correctly, these types of self-test programs can quickly identify faulty areas of the processor. Of course, a certain minimum level of the processor must be functional in order to even begin executing a self-test program. For instance, the basic fetch-execute cycle must be working to be able to read instructions from memory into the IR and begin executing them. It also is necessary for at least some of the conditional branch instructions and the compare instructions to be working properly to be able to determine if at least some of the initial self-tests functioned correctly.

The basic idea behind writing self-test programs is to assume that the absolute minimum level of functionality is correct from the beginning. A short sequence of simple instructions then is used to verify the most basic operations. Once this basic level of execution is verified, additional instructions are checked one-by-one. As additional instructions are verified, they can be used to construct more elaborate instruction sequences to verify more and more complex operations. Thus, you begin by assuming that almost nothing works. Then you slowly verify additional instructions until, at the end, you have thoroughly verified every instruction using a variety of reasonable combinations of inputs.

To demonstrate this type of self-test process, we will describe the simple self-test program developed to verify the original VeSPA behavioral model and its corresponding assembler. This self-test program is by no means complete. However, it does demonstrate the basic principles used to develop this type of program.

8.2.1   Initial steps

Before we can thoroughly verify all of the instructions defined in the ISA, we must choose a very small subset of basic instructions that are necessary for any subsequent testing. At a minimum, we need to be able to load values into a register, we need to be able to compare the results produced by an operation with the expected results, and we need to be able to make a decision based on the result of the comparison. It also would be a good idea to stop the processor if our initial test fails. In the VeSPA processor, we can perform these four types of operations with the load-immediate (`ldi`), compare (`cmp`), conditional branch (`bxx`), and halt (`hlt`) instructions.

With the above observations in mind, we develop the following sequence of instructions as our basic, initial test of VeSPA:

```
ldi r0,#0xf
cmp r0, #15
beq start
hlt             ; if you ended up here, not much is working
```

The first instruction in this sequence loads an arbitrary value into register `r0`. The next instruction compares the value we think we moved into `r0` to the value that was actually loaded. The third instruction then makes a decision based on the outcome of this comparison using the conditional branch instruction.

If the branch instruction itself does not work, the program will fall through to the `hlt` instruction. Furthermore, if the two values do not match, the branch will again fall through to the `hlt` instruction. In either situation, this action likely means that not much of the processor is working properly. We hope that at least the `hlt` instruction is working! If none of these four instructions are working properly, there is no way to determine what will happen next. It is likely, though, that the processor will hang and nothing will happen.

If this simple sequence of instructions executes correctly, though, we will have verified that the fetch-execute cycle seems to be working, that the processor can perform a simple data movement operation, that it can compare two values, and that it can do a simple conditional branch. This is not a very complete test of these operations, of course. We simply verified that the processor could test a single value. It is certainly possible that it might be able to manipulate this particular value, but no others. Or it may work fine for most values, but not all. We also do not know if any registers other than r0 appear to be working properly. Nevertheless, this simple test is enough to begin the self-testing process for the VeSPA processor.

8.2.2   Program structure

It is useful to pause for a moment and describe the overall structure of the test program itself. The basic goal of this structure is to make it easy for the programmer to determine what type of error occurred when an error is detected, or to quickly determine that the program executed correctly from the beginning to the end. If the very simple test described above fails, we hope that the processor will halt at the hlt instruction. Since this is the fourth instruction in the program, the PC will have the value 4 when the program terminates. Thus, if the processor halts with this address in the PC, we know that it did not even complete the most basic operations.

However, if it executes beyond this point in the program, we can use the compare and load instructions to provide a slightly more sophisticated way of communicating to the programmer how well the test progressed. In particular, we set up the following sequence of operations at the end of the test program:

```
; The start of the tests.
start: ...
...
; The end of the tests.

    ldi r0,#good_exit
    jmp r0
error_exits:

error_regs:
    ldi r0,#0x2
    hlt

error_add:
    ldi r0,#0x3
    hlt

error_sub:
    ldi r0,#0x4
```

```
  hlt
...

  .org 0x1000
good_exit:
  ldi r0,#-1
  hlt
```

If all of the tests complete successfully, the program will run to the comment
; The end of the tests. The next instructions it executes will cause it to jump
to the address at the label good_exit. The instructions at this location load the
value −1 into register r0 and then halts. By observing the values in r0 and the PC
when the simulation halts, we can determine if the test was successful or not.

This basic idea of gradually testing more and more instructions allows us to
build a very complex test program that can evaluate the functionality of every
major component within the system. A rather complete program written in VeSPA's
assembly language for performing this type of self-test process is available on the
companion web site.

8.3   Formal verification

The simulation-based verification approaches described in this chapter are somewhat informal and ad hoc. The field of *formal verification*, in contrast, attempts to
further automate the verification process using *theorem proving*-based techniques.
Equivalence checking, for instance, compares the design being tested to a known-good
reference design by mathematically transforming one design to the other. If a sequence
of mathematical transformations can be found that links the two designs, they are said
to be equivalent. Since the design being tested now has been shown to be equivalent
to a known-good design, we can be assured that new design is correct.

Another formal verification technique is called *model checking*. This approach
attempts to prove a set of logical assertions about a design. For instance, the designer
may specify as an input assertion that the memory *read* and *write* signals can
never both be asserted at the same time. Additional assertions can be generated
by the designer from the ISA specification, for instance. The model checker then
attempts to prove automatically that these assertions *must* be true given the specific
implementation of the system.

These formal verification techniques typically are faster and more thorough than
conventional simulation-based approaches. However, there is no guarantee that the
transformation process or the assertion prover will actually terminate successfully.
As a result, there still is a great need for simulation-based verification.

8.4   Summary

The design of any system is not complete until it has been rigorously verified. In this chapter, we have learned about two important techniques for automating the verification process: test benches, and self-test programs.

A test bench is a Verilog program that is used to verify the operation of a hardware module, which also is written in Verilog. The primary operations performed by a test bench program are:

1. generate the *test vectors* used to drive the inputs of the device being tested;
2. apply these test vectors to the device;
3. simulate the operation of the device with these inputs applied;
4. capture the outputs the device produces;
5. compare these outputs to the expected values;
6. report when the simulated output values do not match the expected output values.

The test vectors used as the input stimulus in a test bench program can be generated either manually or automatically using a constrained pseudorandom test vector generator. The real power of a test bench program is that it can partially automate the verification process.

Self-test programs are used as a next step beyond test benches. Self-test programs are written in a high-level programming language, or directly in the processor's assembly language. As the self-test program is executed on the processor being tested, it automatically verifies the correct operation of each instruction. Self-test programs can be used to verify a system while it is being designed. They also can be used on operating systems after the design is complete to verify that an actual hardware device is operating correctly. Finally, we note that more sophisticated techniques, such as equivalence checking and model checking, are often used to bring greater mathematical rigor to the verification process.

Further reading

D. R. Smith and P. D. Franzon, *Verilog Styles for Synthesis of Digital Systems*. Upper Saddle River, NJ: Prentice Hall, 2000. *See in particular Chapter 7.*

A The VeSPA instruction set architecture (ISA)

The instruction set architecture (ISA) of the VeSPA (*Very Small Processor Architecture*) defines the interface between the hardware designer and the assembly language programmer. It consists of all of the programmer accessible storage, plus all of the instructions.

A.1 Notational conventions

The following notation is used in this appendix to describe the ISA.

- **#**. This symbol is used to identify an immediate operand.
- **rdst**. One of the general-purpose registers that will be used as the destination to store the result produced by an instruction.
- **rs1, rs2**. One of the general-purpose registers that will be used as a source value in an operation.
- **rst**. The register that will be written to memory in a store operation.
- **R[rx]**. The contents of general-purpose register rx.
- **Mem[x]**. The contents of memory location x.
- **immedX**. An X-bit immediate value used as a literal.
- **LABEL**. Used in the assembler to symbolically specify a memory location, that is, by name.
- **;**. Used in the assembler to mark the beginning of a comment.
- **sext(x)**. Sign-extend the value x by replicating the sign bit as many times as necessary to extend x to a 32-bit value.
- **setcc(x)**. Set the condition code bits according to the value x.

A.2   Storage elements

The following storage elements are defined in the ISA and are accessible to the assembly language programmer, either directly or indirectly as a side effect of some instructions.

- **Memory**. The main memory consists of 2^{32} locations, each of which is eight-bits wide. The memory uses a big-endian organization so that the most-significant byte of a 32-bit value is stored at the smaller memory address.
- **General-purpose registers**. There are thirty-two 32-bit general-purpose registers available to the programmer. They are numbered from 0 to 31 and given the names r0, r1, r2, $\cdots$, r31.
- **Condition code bits**. The condition code bits, C, V, Z, and N, are set by the result of certain ALU operations and are used by the conditional branch instruction. The C bit indicates that a carry-out from the most significant bit position has occurred; the V bit indicates a carry-out from the sign bit (i.e., overflow of a two's-complement operation); the Z bit is set when the result is zero; and the N bit is set when the result is a negative value (i.e., when the sign bit of the result is 1).
- **Program counter (PC)**. A 32-bit register that points to the *next* instruction to be executed.
- **Instruction register (IR)**. A 32-bit register that holds the instruction being executed. This register cannot be directly accessed by the programmer.

A.3   The instruction specifications

The operations available in the VeSPA ISA are listed below.

Mnemonic	Opcode		Operation
	Decimal	Binary	
NOP	0	00000	No operation.
ADD*	1	00001	Addition.
SUB*	2	00010	Subtraction.
OR	3	00011	Bit-wise logical OR.
AND	4	00100	Bit-wise logical AND.
NOT	5	00101	Bit-wise logical complement.
XOR	6	00110	Bit-wise exclusive-OR.
CMP*	7	00111	Arithmetic comparison.
Bxx†	8	01000	Conditional branch (xx = specific condition).

Mnemonic	Opcode		Operation
	Decimal	Binary	
JMP	9	01001	Jump indirectly through a register + offset.
JMPL	9	01001	Jump and link indirectly through a register + offset.
LD	10	01010	Load direct from memory.
LDI	11	01011	Load an immediate value.
LDX	12	01100	Load indirect through index register + offset.
ST	13	01101	Store direct to memory.
STX	14	01110	Store indirect through index register + offset.
HLT	31	11111	Halt execution.

Assembler pseudo-operations.

MOV*		Move (actually copy) one register to another.

* These instructions set the condition code bits.
† This instruction reads the condition code bits.

The following describes the operation of each of these instructions in detail. Also included is the instruction encoding, the appropriate assembler syntax, and some assembly language examples.

ADD* – Addition

*This instruction sets the condition code bits.

Assembly code notation

    a) ADD rdst, rs1, rs2
    b) ADD rdst, rs1, #immed16

Instruction encoding

a)

31 ⋯ 27	26 ⋯ 22	21 ⋯ 17	16	15 ⋯ 11	10 ⋯ 0
00001	rdst	rs1	0	rs2	000 0000 0000

b)

31 ⋯ 27	26 ⋯ 22	21 ⋯ 17	16	15 ⋯ 0
00001	rdst	rs1	1	immed16

Description

The ADD instruction adds the two source operands and stores the result in the destination register specified by rdst. One of the operands is always taken from the register pointed to by rs1. If IR[16] == 0, the second operand is taken from the register pointed to by rs2. If IR[16] == 1, however, the second operand is the literal value obtained by sign-extending the 16-bit immediate field, immed16, to 32 bits. The condition code values are set according to the result produced by the addition operation.

Detailed operation

```
if (IR[16] == 0)
    R[rdst] ← R[rs1] + R[rs2];
else
    R[rdst] ← R[rs1] + sext(immed16);
setcc(R[rdst]);
PC ← PC + 4;
```

Assembly code examples

```
ADD r2, r3, r5     ; store the sum of r3 and r5 into r2
ADD r6, r8, #98    ; store into r6 the sum of r8 and 98
```

AND – Bit-wise logical AND

Assembly code notation

    a) AND rdst, rs1, rs2
    b) AND rdst, rs1, #immed16

Instruction encoding

a)

31 ··· 27	26 ··· 22	21 ··· 17	16	15 ··· 11	10 ··· 0
00100	rdst	rs1	0	rs2	000 0000 0000

b)

31 ··· 27	26 ··· 22	21 ··· 17	16	15 ··· 0
00100	rdst	rs1	1	immed16

Description

The AND instruction forms the logical AND of the two source operands and stores the result in the destination register specified by rdst. One of the operands is always taken from the register pointed to by rs1. If IR[16] == 0, the second operand is taken from the register pointed to by rs2. If IR[16] == 1, however, the second operand is the literal value obtained by sign-extending the 16-bit immediate field, immed16, to 32 bits.

Detailed operation

```
if (IR[16] == 0)
        R[rdst] ← R[rs1] AND R[rs2];
else
        R[rdst] ← R[rs1] AND sext(immed16);
PC ← PC + 4;
```

Assembly code examples

```
AND r2, r3, r5    ; store the logical AND of r3 and r5 into r2
AND r6, r8, #98   ; store into r6 the logical AND of r8 and 98
```

Bxx – Conditional branch

This instruction reads the condition code bits.

Assembly code notation

Bxx LABEL ; where xx corresponds to a specific condition to test

Instruction encoding

31 ⋯ 27	26 ⋯ 23	22 ⋯ 0
01000	cond	immed23

where cond is one of the following values:

cond	Assembly	Condition
0000	BRA	branch always
1000	BNV	branch never
0001	BCC	branch on carry clear ($\bar{C}$)
1001	BCS	branch on carry set (C)
0010	BVC	branch on overflow clear ($\bar{V}$)
1010	BVS	branch on overflow set (V)
0011	BEQ	branch on equal (Z)
1011	BNE	branch on not equal ($\bar{Z}$)
0100	BGE	branch on greater than or equal to ($\bar{N}\bar{V}|NV$)
1100	BLT	branch on less than ($N\bar{V}|\bar{N}V$)
0101	BGT	branch on greater than ($\bar{Z}(\bar{N}\bar{V}|NV)$)
1101	BLE	branch on less than or equal to ($Z|(N\bar{V}|\bar{N}V)$)
0110	BPL	branch on plus (positive) ($\bar{N}$)
1110	BMI	branch on minus (negative) (N)

Description

If the specified condition evaluates to true, this instruction will branch to the target address. If the condition evaluates to false, the instruction immediately following the branch is executed.

The target address is determined by adding the sign-extended value of the immed23 field to the current value of the program counter, thereby implementing a PC-relative branch operation. Note that, while the branch instruction is being executed, the PC value is pointing to the instruction after the branch instruction. Thus, the assembler must calculate the literal value to be stored in the immed23 field as follows: immed23 = address_of(LABEL) − (PC + 4).

To evaluate the condition, the branch instruction reads the condition code bits and forms the corresponding logical expression shown in the above table. These condition codes are set by the most recent instruction that used the ALU. They indicate the various arithmetic relationships that exist after the operation X−Y, where X and Y are signed two's-complement integers.

Detailed operation

```
if (condition == 1)
        PC ← PC + 4 + sext(immed23);
else
        PC ← PC + 4;
```

where *condition* is the result of computing the logic equations shown in the above table.

Assembly code examples

```
CMP r2, r3    ; compare r2 and r3 to set the condition codes
BGE LABEL     ; branch to LABEL if r2 is greater than or equal to r3
```

CMP* – Compare

*This instruction sets the condition code bits.

Assembly code notation

a) CMP rs1, rs2
b) CMP rs1, #value

Instruction encoding

a)

31 ⋯ 27	26 ⋯ 22	21 ⋯ 17	16	15 ⋯ 11	10 ⋯ 0
00111	00000	rs1	0	rs2	000 0000 0000

b)

31 ⋯ 27	26 ⋯ 22	21 ⋯ 17	16	15 ⋯ 0
00111	00000	rs1	1	immed16

Description

The CMP instruction compares the operand values by subtracting the second operand from the first operand. The result of this subtraction is used to set the condition code bits. The result itself is not stored. One of the operands is always taken from the register pointed to by rs1. If IR[16] == 0, the second operand is taken from the register pointed to by rs2. If IR[16] == 1, however, the second operand is the literal value obtained by sign-extending the 16-bit immediate field, immed16, to 32 bits.

Detailed operation

```
if (IR[16] == 0)
        setcc(R[rs1] - R[rs2]);
else
        setcc(R[rs1] - sext(immed16));
PC ← PC + 4;
```

Assembly code examples

```
CMP r2, r3      ; Set the condition codes that result from computing
                  R[r2] - R[r3]
CMP r2, #98     ; Set the condition codes that result from computing
                  R[r2] - 98
```

HLT – Halt

Assembly code notation

HLT

Instruction encoding

31 ⋯ 27	26 ⋯ 0
11111	000 0000 0000 0000 0000 0000 0000

Description

Stop execution.

Detailed operation

None

Assembly code examples

```
HLT
```

JMP – Jump indirect + offset

JMPL – Jump and link indirect + offset

Assembly code notation

    a) JMP rs1, #value

    b) JMPL rdst, rs1, #value

Instruction encoding

a)

31 ⋯ 27	26 ⋯ 22	21 ⋯ 17	16	15 ⋯ 0
01001	00000	rs1	0	immed16

b)

31 ⋯ 27	26 ⋯ 22	21 ⋯ 17	16	15 ⋯ 0
01001	rdst	rs1	1	immed16

Description

Unconditionally jump to the address specified by adding the contents of register rs1 with the literal value found by sign-extending immed16. If $IR[16] == 1$ (i.e., the link bit is set), also store the current value of the PC, which is the address of the instruction following the jump, in register rdst.

Detailed operation

```
if (IR[16] == 1)
      R[rdst] ← PC;
PC ← R[rs1] + sext(immed16);
```

Assembly code examples

```
JMP r10              ; jump to the address stored in r10
JMP r16,#39          ; jump to the address (R[r10] + 39)
JMPL r31, r10        ; jump to the address stored in r10,
                     ; and save the return address in r31
JMPL r31,r16,#39     ; jump to the address (R[r16] + 39),
                     ; and save the return address in r31
```

LD – Load direct

Assembly code notation

    LD rdst, LABEL

Instruction encoding

31 ⋯ 27	26 ⋯ 22	21 ⋯ 0
01010	rdst	immed22

Description

Read the memory location specified by the sign-extended literal field immed22 and store the result in register `rdst`.

Detailed operation

```
R[rdst] ← Mem[sext(immed22)];
PC ← PC + 4;
```

Assembly code examples

```
LD r6, LABEL ; load the value at LABEL into r6
```

LDI – Load immediate

Assembly code notation

```
LDI rdst, #value
```

Instruction encoding

31 ⋯ 27	26 ⋯ 22	21 ⋯ 0
01011	rdst	immed22

Description

Move the sign-extended literal field immed22 into register `rdst`.

Detailed operation

```
R[rdst] ← sext(immed22);
PC ← PC + 4;
```

Assembly code examples

```
LDI r6, #45        ; move the value 45 into r6
LDI r13, #LABEL    ; move the address of LABEL into r13
```

LDX – Load indexed

Assembly code notation

```
LDX rdst, rs1
LDX rdst, rs1, #value
```

Instruction encoding

31 ··· 27	26 ··· 22	21 ··· 17	16 ··· 0
01100	rdst	rs1	immed17

Description

Read the memory location specified by adding the contents of register rs1 and the sign-extended literal field immed17. Store this value in register rdst.

Detailed operation

```
R[rdst] ← Mem[R[rs1] + sext(immed17)];
PC ← PC + 4;
```

Assembly code examples

```
LDX r6,r8        ; load the value at the address in r8 into r6
LDX r6,r8, #46   ; load the value at the address (R[r8] + 46) into r6
```

MOV* – Move register to register

*This instruction sets the condition code bits.

Assembly code notation

MOV rdst, rs1

Instruction encoding

31 ··· 27	26 ··· 22	21 ··· 17	16	15 ··· 0
00001	rdst	rs1	1	0000 0000 0000 0000

Description

Move (actually, copy) the contents of register rs1 to register rdst. MOV is really a pseudo-operation that the assembler converts to the equivalent instruction ADD rdst, rs1, #0. The condition code values are set according to the value moved.

Detailed operation

```
R[rdst] ← R[rs1];
setcc(R[rdst]);
PC ← PC + 4;
```

Assembly code examples

```
MOV r2, r3 ; copy the contents of r3 into r2
```

NOP – No-operation

Assembly code notation

NOP

Instruction encoding

31 ⋯ 27	26 ⋯ 0
00000	000 0000 0000 0000 0000 0000 0000

Description

Perform no-operation, except for incrementing the PC to point to the next instruction to execute.

Detailed operation

PC ← PC + 4;

Assembly code examples

NOP

NOT – Bit-wise logical complement

Assembly code notation

a) NOT rdst, rs1

Instruction encoding

31 ⋯ 27	26 ⋯ 22	21 ⋯ 17	16 ⋯ 0
00101	rdst	rs1	0 0000 0000 0000 0000

Description

Form the logical complement of the value in register rs1 and store the result in register rdst.

Detailed operation

R[rdst] ← NOT(R[rs1]);
PC ← PC + 4;

Assembly code examples

NOT r2, r3,; put the complement of r3 into r2

OR – Bit-wise logical OR

Assembly code notation

      a) OR rdst, rs1, rs2

      b) OR rdst, rs1, #immed16

Instruction encoding

a)

31 ⋯ 27	26 ⋯ 22	21 ⋯ 17	16	15 ⋯ 11	10 ⋯ 0
00011	rdst	rs1	0	rs2	000 0000 0000

b)

31 ⋯ 27	26 ⋯ 22	21 ⋯ 17	16	15 ⋯ 0
00011	rdst	rs1	1	immed16

Description

The OR instruction forms the logical OR of the two source operands and stores the result in the destination register specified by rdst. One of the operands is always taken from the register pointed to by rs1. If IR[16] == 0, the second operand is taken from the register pointed to by rs2. If IR[16] == 1, however, the second operand is the literal value obtained by sign-extending the 16-bit immediate field, immed16, to 32 bits.

Detailed operation

```
if (IR[16] == 0)
        R[rdst] ← R[rs1] OR R[rs2];
else
        R[rdst] ← R[rs1] OR sext(immed16);
PC ← PC + 4;
```

Assembly code examples

```
OR r2, r3, r5      ; store the logical OR of r3 and r5 into r2
OR r6, r8, #98     ; store into r6 the logical OR of r8 and 98
```

ST – Store direct

Assembly code notation

      ST LABEL, rst

Instruction encoding

31 ⋯ 27	26 ⋯ 22	21 ⋯ 0
01101	rst	immed22

Description

Store register `rst` into the memory location specified by the sign-extended literal field immed22.

Detailed operation

```
Mem[ sext( immed22 ) ] ← R[ rst ];
PC ← PC + 4;
```

Assembly code examples

```
ST LABEL, r6 ; store r6 at the memory location LABEL
```

STX – Store indexed

Assembly code notation

```
STX rs1, rst
STX rs1, #value, rst
```

Instruction encoding

31 ⋯ 27	26 ⋯ 22	21 ⋯ 17	16 ⋯ 0
01110	rst	rs1	immed17

Description

Store the value in register `rst` into the memory location specified by adding the contents of register `rs1` and the sign-extended literal field immed17.

Detailed operation

```
Mem[ R[ rs1 ] + sext( immed17 ) ] ← R[ rst ];
PC ← PC + 4;
```

Assembly code examples

```
STX r8,r6        ; store r6 in memory at the address in r8
STX r8,#46,r6    ; store r6 in memory at the address (R[ r8 ] + 46)
```

SUB* – Subtraction

*This instruction sets the condition code bits.

Assembly code notation
a) SUB rdst, rs1, rs2
b) SUB rdst, rs1, #immed16

Instruction encoding

a)

31 ··· 27	26 ··· 22	21 ··· 17	16	15 ··· 11	10 ··· 0
00010	rdst	rs1	0	rs2	000 0000 0000

b)

31 ··· 27	26 ··· 22	21 ··· 17	16	15 ··· 0
00010	rdst	rs1	1	immed16

Description

The SUB instruction subtracts the two source operands and stores the result in the destination register specified by rdst. The first operand is always taken from the register pointed to by rs1. If IR[16] == 0, the second operand is taken from the register pointed to by rs2. If IR[16] == 1, however, the second operand is the literal value obtained by sign-extending the 16-bit immediate field, immed16, to 32 bits. The condition code values are set according to the result produced by the subtraction operation.

Detailed operation

```
if(IR[16] == 0)
      R[rdst]← R[rs1] – R[rs2];
else
      R[rdst]← R[rs1] – sext(immed16);
setcc(R[rdst]);
PC← PC + 4;
```

Assembly code examples

```
SUB r2, r3, r5     ; store (r3 – r5) into r2
SUB r6, r8, #98    ; store (r8 – 98) into r6
```

XOR – Bit-wise logical exclusive-OR

Assembly code notation
    a) XOR rdst, rs1, rs2
    b) XOR rdst, rs1, #immed16

Instruction encoding

a)

31 ⋯ 27	26 ⋯ 22	21 ⋯ 17	16	15 ⋯ 11	10 ⋯ 0
00110	rdst	rs1	0	rs2	000 0000 0000

b)

31 ⋯ 27	26 ⋯ 22	21 ⋯ 17	16	15 ⋯ 0
00110	rdst	rs1	1	immed16

Description

The XOR instruction forms the logical exclusive-OR of the two source operands and stores the result in the destination register specified by rdst. One of the operands is always taken from the register pointed to by rs1. If IR[16] $==$ 0, the second operand is taken from the register pointed to by rs2. If IR[16] $==$ 1, however, the second operand is the literal value obtained by sign-extending the 16-bit immediate field, immed16, to 32 bits.

Detailed operation

```
if (IR[16] == 0)
      R[rdst] ← R[rs1] XOR R[rs2];
else
      R[rdst] ← R[rs1] XOR sext(immed16);
PC ← PC + 4;
```

Assembly code examples

```
XOR r2, r3, r5    ; store the logical exclusive OR of r3 and r5 into r2
XOR r6, r8, #98   ; store into r6 the logical exclusive OR of r8 and 98
```

The VASM assembler

The assembler developed for the VeSPA processor is called VASM, for VeSPA ASeMbler. This assembler takes a text file as input and produces as output an object file consisting of a sequence of hexadecimal values. The contents of this file can be read into the simulated VeSPA memory by the Verilog simulator using the `readmemh()` operation.

The error-checking in the VASM assembler is not very robust making it all too easy to confuse the assembler. Furthermore, the error messages it produces are very brief and can sometimes be misleading. Nevertheless, it is still easier to use this assembler to produce the object file rather than trying to assemble your programs by hand. This appendix provides a brief summary of the assembler notation. Additionally, Section B.4 shows how to modify the assembler with a detailed example of adding a new instruction.

B.1   Notational conventions

The following notation is interpreted by the assembler to have special meaning.

- **;, //.** Both the semicolon (;) and two adjacent forward slash characters (//) indicate that the following text is a comment. Any characters on a line that follow either of these symbols are ignored by the assembler. These two types of comment characters have identical meanings and can be used interchangeably.
- **#.** The pound sign is used to denote an immediate operand. For example, #58 tells the assembler to use the value 58 as an immediate operand.
- **0x.** This character sequence indicates that the following number should be interpreted as a hexadecimal value. Thus, 0x10 is interpreted as the value 16, while 10 would be interpreted as the value ten.
- **r and R.** Processor registers are identified by the letter r or R followed by an integer value between 0 and 31. For example, r29 is interpreted as register number 29.

- **:**. The colon character appears at the end of an alphanumeric character sequence to indicate that this instance of a symbolic label defines its value. This type of label is used as the target of a branch instruction, for instance, or to symbolically reference a location in the memory.
- **Identifiers**. An *identifier* used as a label consists of a letter followed by zero or more letters, digits, or the underscore character (_). For example, `THE_START_OF_THE_LOOP`, `B`, `a45`, and `vector_23` are all valid identifiers.
- **White-space**. Extra white-space (i.e., tabs, spaces, and newline characters) is ignored by the assembler. This type of white-space is useful for formatting the assembly code to make it more readable.

B.2 Assembler directives

Most of the operations that appear in an assembly language program are translated directly into an equivalent machine instruction. Assembler directives, however, are commands to the assembler itself that force it to perform certain actions. These actions may or may not result in code being generated for the processor. The following directives are available in this assembler.

- **.byte constant**. This directive allocates one byte of memory and initializes it to the given value.

    Example: `MAX_I: .byte 12` allocates a byte of memory with the symbolic name `MAX_I` and initializes it to the value 12.
- **.word constant**. This command allocates one word (four bytes) of memory and initializes it to the given value.

    Example: `SUM: .word 3402` allocates four bytes of memory with the symbolic name `SUM` and initializes it to the value 3402.
- **.alloc constant**. This command is used to allocate a sequence of bytes, each initialized to zero.

    Example: `ARRAY_A: .alloc 100` allocates 100 bytes of memory with the label `ARRAY_A` corresponding to the address of the first byte.
- **.org constant**. This command forces the assembler to begin storing the next sequence of instructions at the given memory address.

    Example: `.org 0x1000` will force the following instructions to be loaded beginning at memory location 0x1000.
- **.equ**. This command assigns a value to an identifier. It typically is used to assign a value to a symbolic constant.

    Example: `LOOPCNT .equ 5` will substitute the value 5 wherever the identifier `LOOPCNT` appears in the program.

B.3   Example program

```
;
; A test program that simply loops 'count' number of times.
; r0 = the value read from the variable 'count'
; r1 = the current iteration number
;
        .org 0          ; start the program at address 0
        ld r0,count     ; load the value of count into r0
        ldi r1,#0       ; initialize r1 to 0
back:   add r1,r1,#1    ; add one to the value in r1
        cmp r1,r0       ; compare the iteration number (r1) to the count (r0)
        ble back        ; loop if r1 <= r0
        hlt             ; otherwise, stop execution
;
; Define the storage locations
;
count:
        .word 0xA       ; number of times to loop (in hex)
```

B.4   Modifying the assembler

The VeSPA assembler, VASM, is constructed using the software tools *lex* and *yacc*. These tools were developed to help compiler writers perform the tedious tasks necessary to convert a program from a textual representation into an internal representation in the compiler's memory that can be used to generate the corresponding object code. These tools are much more powerful than we need to construct a simple two-pass assembler. However, once we have built the assembler, these tools make it relatively straightforward to modify.

In this section, we give a very brief introduction to *lex* and *yacc* by showing how to modify VASM to add a new instruction. The same process also could be used to alter the semantics of an existing instruction, for instance.

Say that we wish to add a mov instruction to the VeSPA processor. This new instruction will move a value from one register to another. However, we would like to minimize the changes that need to be made to both the ISA and the assembler. We realize that we can emulate the operation of a mov instruction by using an add instruction with the value 0 for one of the two input operands. For instance, add r0,r5,#0 will have the same final effect as mov r0,r5. In both cases, the current contents of register r5 will be copied into register r0. Thus, we can add this new instruction to VeSPA by defining the new pseudo-operation, mov. By making the assembler convert the mov operand into an equivalent add instruction, we do not need to change the processor design itself. Instead, all we need to change is the assembler.

B.4.1 Lexical analysis and parsing modifications

The first thing that needs to be changed is to make the assembler's lexical analyzer recognize `mov` as a new token. The file **vasm.lex** contains the *lex* rules used to perform the lexical analysis. Near the beginning of this file, we see several lines similar to the following:

```
add|ADD    {yylval = NONE;    return(ADD);    }
```

This particular line defines a rule that will return the token *ADD* to the parser whenever the the characters `add` or `ADD` occur in the assembler's input. The variable `yylval` can be used to return additional information to the parser, if needed. In this case, we assign it the literal value NONE since we are not returning any additional values.

To make the assembler recognize our new `mov` instruction, we need to add a similar rule to the *lex* file:

```
mov|MOV    {yylval = NONE;    return(MOV);    }
```

This new rule will cause the assembler to return the token *MOV* to the parser whenever the characters `mov` or `MOV` are seen in the input stream.

The next step is to make the assembler's parser recognize statements that contain a `mov` instruction. Each unique token that is to be recognized by the parser must be defined in the file **vasm.yacc**. To declare the new token for `mov`, the following line must be added to the list of tokens defined in this file:

```
%token  MOV
```

The purpose of this definition is simply to tell the parser that *MOV* is to be treated as a token.

We now must define a new parsing rule that describes the order in which the operands will appear in this new instruction, and how they should be interpreted. This rule will be used to insert the operands for this statement into the symbol table, and to insert the statement itself into the list of statements from the assembly code source program. The format of this instruction should be the token `mov` followed by two register identifiers. The register identifiers must be separated by a comma, for example, `move r0,r1`.

A parsing rule in *yacc* that will recognize this new instruction looks like the following:

```
| MOV reg ',' reg
    {
        add_stmt(MOV_OP,ADD_CODE,$2,$4,zero_ptr,REG_TYPE,WORD_SIZE);
    }
```

The vertical bar (|) at the beginning of the rule tells the *yacc* tool that this is one of several possible rules for what a program statement could look like. The parser produced by *yacc* will scan through the list of rules we have defined looking for one that matches the sequence of tokens that have been read in. When it finds a matching rule, it executes the C program statement following the rule between the braces.

The above rule that we have defined for the new mov instruction will be matched when the input sequence of tokens is the MOV token followed by a register specifier, a comma, and another register specifier. The register specifiers are identified with the reg rule. This rule is defined later in the file vasm.yacc to be either of the characters R or r followed by a number between 0 and 31. When this rule is matched, the C function call add_stmt will be executed.

This function call is defined at the end of the vasm.yacc file. Its primary operation is to add the parameters into an array of structures that forms a list of all of the noncomment statements in the assembly language program being processed. The parameters that will be stored are determined by the above parsing rule for MOV. The first parameter is a tag that identifies the statement as a mov operation. The second parameter is the opcode that is associated with this operation. In this case, we have decided that the mov operation will be translated into an add instruction with the appropriate parameters. Thus, we insert the opcode for the add instruction into this parameter. If we were adding an entirely new instruction to the VeSPA processor, we would insert the corresponding new opcode here instead of the add opcode. In addition, we would have to add a new unique opcode value and name in the file gvars.h and update the ISA specification accordingly.

The next three parameters are the operands for this operation. In the *yacc* tool, a variable name of the form $1 refers to the first token in the corresponding parsing rule. Thus, the variable $1 corresponds to the token MOV, $2 corresponds to the first reg token, $3 corresponds to the comma, and $4 corresponds to the second reg token. Since we want the two register specifiers to be used by the mov operation, we insert the $2 and $4 variables into the first two of the three operand parameter positions in add_stmt function call. The last parameter should always be 0 for the mov operation, so we insert the variable zero_ptr for this parameter. This variable has been previously defined to be a pointer into the symbol table for the constant value 0.

Finally, the last two parameters in the add_stmt function call specify the addressing mode used in the instruction (register-to-register) and the number of bytes that this instruction requires (four bytes, or one word).

With these additions to the *lex* and *yacc* files, we have now added the mov operation to the first pass of the assembler. It will now recognize statements of the form mov r5,r9, for example. An appropriate entry into the list of program statements then will be made for this instruction every time it is encountered in the assembly language source code file.

B.4.2   Code generation modifications

The final addition to VASM that must be made is to add the `mov` operation to the code generation pass. This pass is in the file `codegen.c`. The main loop in this pass scans through the internal representation of each statement found in the first pass. A `switch` statement is used to select the appropriate section for generating the machine language code for each statement individually. Consequently, we need to insert a new `case` for the `mov` operation, as follows:

```
case MOV_OP:
    code = 0;
    code |= (0x1f & stmt[i].op_code) << 27;
    code |= (0x1f & sym_table[stmt[i].op1].value) << 22;
    code |= (0x1f & sym_table[stmt[i].op2].value) << 17;
    code |= 1 << 16;
    print_code(code,4,&lc);
    break;
```

The variable `code` will eventually contain the final machine language code for this statement. This is the value that will be written to the object file. After initializing it to 0, we insert the appropriate values for each field in the instruction using the C language logical OR with assignment operator, $|=$. Since we are implementing the `mov` operation using an add instruction, the appropriate fields are those defined for the add instruction in the ISA, as shown in Appendix A. The first field to be set is the opcode, which was initialized to the appropriate value in the `stmt[i].op_code` variable during the first pass of the assembler. The left shift by 27 bits operation (<< 27) moves the five opcode bits into the most significant bit positions. The next two statements insert the operand register numbers into the appropriate fields using the shift operator and the logical OR operator. The statement `code |= 1 << 16` inserts a 1 into bit 16 to indicate that the second operand is an immediate value, as defined in the ISA. This operand value was already initialized to 0 when the variable `code` was initialized at the start of the `case`. The last statement in this `case` prints the generated machine code for this assembly language statement to the output file.

With these simple changes, we have now added a new `mov` pseudo-operation to VASM. This new operation now can be used in any VASM assembly language program just like any other type of instruction.

Further reading

This book provides a comprehensive explanation of how to use the *lex* and *yacc* programming tools. It is accessible to both beginners and advanced users.

A. Mason, J. Levine, and D. Brown, *lex & yacc*, 2nd ed. O'Reilly and Associates, 1992.

Index

VeSPA Instruction Set

Mnemonic	Opcode		Operation
	Decimal	Binary	
NOP	0	00000	No operation
ADD	1	00001	Addition
SUB	2	00010	Subtraction
OR	3	00011	Bit-wise logical OR
AND	4	00100	Bit-wise logical AND
NOT	5	00101	Bit-wise logical complement
XOR	6	00110	Bit-wise exclusive-OR
CMP	7	00111	Arithmetic comparison
Bxx	8	01000	Conditional branch (xx = condition)
JMP	9	01001	Jump indirectly through a register + offset
JMPL	9	01001	Jump and link indirectly through a register + offset
LD	10	01010	Load direct from memory
LDI	11	01011	Load an immediate value
LDX	12	01100	Load indirect through index register + offset
ST	13	01101	Store direct to memory
STX	14	01110	Store indirect through index register + offset
HLT	31	11111	Halt execution
Assembler pseudo-operations			
MOV	1	00001	Move (copy) one register to another. This instruction actually is a pseudo-op that is converted to an ADD by the assembler.

VeSPA Instruction format

Bit position / Instruction	31...27	26...23	22	21...17	16	15...11	10...0
ADD, AND, CMP*, OR, SUB, XOR (register-to-register)	opcode	rdst		rs1	0	rs2	0...0
ADD, AND, CMP*, OR, SUB, XOR (immediate operand)	opcode	rdst		rs1	1	immed16	
Conditional branch	opcode	condition bits	immed23				
HALT, NOP	opcode	0...0					
JMP	opcode	00000		rs1	0	immed16	
JMPL	opcode	rdst		rs1	1	immed16	
LD, LDI	opcode	rdst	immed22				
LDX	opcode	rdst		rs1	immed17		
MOV	opcode	rdst		rs1	1	0...0	
NOT	opcode	rdst		rs1	0...0		
ST	opcode	rst	immed22				
STX	opcode	rst		rs1	immed17		

*The rdst field for the CMP instruction is not used and should be set to 00000.

VeSPA Branch conditions

Condition bits	Mnemonic	Condition tested
0000	BRA	Branch always
1000	BNV	Branch never
0001	BCC	Branch on carry clear
1001	BCS	Branch on carry set
0010	BVC	Branch on overflow clear
1010	BVS	Branch on overflow set
0011	BEQ	Branch on equal
1011	BNE	Branch on not equal
0100	BGE	Branch on greater than or equal to
1100	BLT	Branch on less than
0101	BGT	Branch on greater than
1101	BLE	Branch on less than or equal to
0110	BPL	Branch on plus (positive value)
1110	BMI	Branch on minus (negative value)

Verilog operators

Arithmetic operators

Operator	Add	Subtract	Multiply	Divide	Modulus
Symbol	+	−	*	/	%

Logical, bit-wise, and reduction operators

Operator	Boolean			Bit-wise Boolean				
	and	or	not	and	or	not	xor	xnor
Symbol	&&	||	!	&	|	~	^	~^

Relational operators

Operator	greater than	less than	greater than or equal to	less than or equal to	equal	not equal	equal (case)	not equal (case)
Symbol	>	<	>=	<=	==	!=	===	!===

Miscellaneous operators

Operator	left shift	right shift	concatenation	replication
Symbol	<<	>>	{X, Y}	{X{Y}}

Conditional operator

condition ? : true_consequence : false_consequence

Format specifications used in the Verilog *$display* task

Format specifiers	
%b	Binary value
%c	Single ASCII character
%d	Decimal value
%h	Hexadecimal value
%m	A hierarchical name
%o	Octal value
%s	String of ASCII characters
%t	Verilog-defined global time value
%s	Signal strength value of a net
Character escape sequences	
\n	Newline
\t	Tab
%%	The % character
\"	The "character
\\	The \ character